tales for topics

Linking favourite stories with popular topics for children aged five to nine

Stephanie Mudd and Hilary Mason

Line drawings by Kathie Barrs

Children's work and displays organised
by Barbara Hume, Sophie Allen,
Helen Gwynne and Katie Kitching

First published in 1993 by
BELAIR PUBLICATIONS LIMITED
P.O. Box 12, Twickenham, TW1 2QL England,

© Stephanie Mudd and Hilary Mason

Series Editor Robyn Gordon
Designed by Richard Souper
Photography by Kelvin Freeman
Typesetting by Belair
Printed and Bound by Heanor Gate Printing Ltd

ISBN 0 947882 25 1

D0412551

Acknowledgements

The Authors and Publishers would like to thank the teachers and children of East Sheen Primary School, Richmond-upon-Thames, for their invaluable contributions in the preparation of classroom displays: with special thanks to Barbara Hume, Sophie Allen, Helen Gwynne and Katie Kitching.

They would also like to give their grateful thanks to Ibstock Place, The Froebel School, London SWI5, for permission to use the photograph of the school's patchwork wall-hanging on page 29; and to Meryl Gray for the cover artwork.

The Authors would also like to thank Marilyn Brocklehurst and staff at the Norfolk Children's Book Centre for their unflagging help and an inspiring range of wonderful children's books.

Contents

Introduction

Teachers have always recognised that sharing a good book with the children is one of the best ways of stimulating an interest in a topic. This book recommends some high-quality children's fiction which can provide a meaningful context for topic activities.

For each of the 22 topics, we have suggested some good books for you to enjoy with the children. One book is highlighted for each topic, but we have also suggested some others which support the themes just as well. The topic activities will work with any of the recommended books you use.

The topic activities cover National Curriculum subjects: English, maths, science, design and technology; humanities; art and craft; music. Based on the Programmes of Study, they are designed to support a broad and balanced curriculum.

At the beginning of each topic, under the heading 'Collections' we have suggested some materials you might like to collect, which could be used to set up a hands-on display. Encourage the children to add their own contributions as you go along.

Under the heading 'Starters', there are some introductory ideas for launching the topic, and for using the collection materials. These initial ideas provide opportunities for discussion, activities and games, building on what the children may already know.

The final section of each topic suggests some 'Further activities from the book'. These are often still related to the major theme, but give additional ideas which spring directly from the highlighted story.

The activities offer lots of scope for children of different ages and abilities. With some children, you may feel it appropriate to go no further than the 'look at and talk about stage', while other children could be encouraged to explore further. You know your children best - work at their level, selecting from the bank of activities to suit individual needs.

There is no emphasis here on 'studying' the books. A story has its own reason for being; it doesn't exist merely to support classroom topics. Often you will want to do no more with a book than read and enjoy it with the children.

There is a treasure trove of brilliant children's fiction on the market. It is incredibly hard to choose; there are always other books you wish you had the space to include. Luckily, in the classroom you are not subjected to the same restrictions. Choose what you and the children really enjoy reading. The aim is to immerse children in high quality fiction, and purposeful activities.

Stephanie Mudd and Hilary Mason

The authors and publishers have made every effort to ensure that the suggested titles are available through bookshops, school and county libraries

Post Office

Choose a character and plot the Jolly Postman's route to that character's house

THE JOLLY POSTMAN, J. and A. Ahlberg (Heinemann)
Katie Morag delivers the mail, Mairi Hedderwick. *A Letter for Tiger,* Janosch.
Dear Daddy, Philippe Dupasquier. *Deathwood Letters,* Hazel Townson.

Collections

Post office materials (see English/Role Play). A range of forms of writing sent through the post: letters, greetings and post cards, bills, leaflets. Envelopes of different shapes/sizes including padded bags and post office approved boxes. Stamps of various shapes, sizes and countries. Writing materials: quills, fountain pens, biros, felt-tip pens. Local street map.

Starters

Discuss the kinds of things the children have received through the post. Don't forget mail order, flowers, parcels. Why do we pay postage? Why are there first and second class stamps, and why do parcels cost more than letters to send? Make stamp-shaped vocabulary cards: parcel, paper, postman, sorting office, franking machine, telex. Compile a class directory of important telephone contact numbers. Make a stamp scrap book: how can they be grouped (sports, flowers, special issues)? Read out different kinds of letters to give the children a flavour of the sorts of messages we send through the post. Look at writing scripts used on envelopes: typed, cursive, different alphabets.

English/Role Play

● Use toy/old phones to practise inviting a friend over to play, ringing a parent at work, making emergency calls.
● Set up a post office. You could include: scales, clock, stamp sheets, charts of postal rates (inland and overseas), cash register, collection sack, sorting area, telephone and directory, information leaflets, savings and pension books. Role play postman, counter clerk and customer to practise money work.

- Have your own internal post system. Write to people in school: thank you to the cook for the special meal; congratulations on an enjoyable assembly/production; letters to friends in other classes. Try using a letter format on a word processor.
- Make up a message for an answering machine for the class, home, school office.
- To practise addresses, get the children to write home with invitations, reminders etc. The addresses could be stored in a card file, on a data bank, or on sticky labels for younger children.
- Sort old envelopes into alphabetical order by name, street or post code.
- Use telephone books, Yellow Pages (or your own simplified versions) to practise research skills such as alphabetical order and sub headings.
- Have a quiz: find a local music shop or the address of a favourite local charity.

Maths

- Envelopes: sort by colour, size, shape, number or value of stamps. Estimate, then measure, height, width, perimeters. Look at nets and make your own on squared paper.

- Make shape pictures of a post office van, post box or telephone kiosk with used stamps or ('stamp' shapes). Record how many of each stamp were used in the picture. Older children could work out the total value of their picture. Make one worth more than/less than the original.

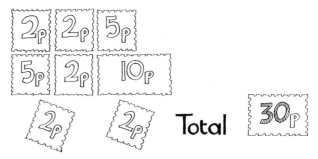

- Direct a Roamer/Turtle 'post van' along a simple delivery route. Start with a straight street, add crossroads, or make a representation of your locality. Alternatively, use a screen turtle.
- Make up 'parcels' of different weights. Can the children order them from lightest to heaviest? Work out how much it would cost to send some of the parcels using Post Office parcel rates or your own prices.
- Guess my house number. Take turns guessing the child's house number by asking questions like: is it more than/less than 12? Is it an odd number? Does it have the figure 9 in it? Use a number line/square after each question to blank off which numbers it cannot be.
- Using only 3p and 5p stamps, how many different totals can you make? Make a table of your findings.
- Make a tally chart or frequency graph of incoming school post. Estimate how many letters will be received in a day/week/month and compare with your findings.

Science

- Find the most efficient way of sealing parcels. Give the children a selection from: parcel tape, adhesive tape, PVA glue, string, ribbons, wax seal. Which is the easiest to apply/remove? Give each method a score out of 10. Investigate different combinations e.g. adhesive tape and string.
- Test the absorbency of different kinds of paper. Use felt-tips to draw a post box on different kinds of paper (blotting, tissue, grease-proof, cartridge etc). Display findings by labelling each type of paper and ordering them from easiest/clearest to draw on, to the most unclear.
- Investigate different ways of water-proofing an address label. Try adhesive tape, wax, oil, clear plastic, nail varnish. Set and display the labels as a probability line - those that will never find their destinations, those which have a good chance and those most likely to arrive.
- Test the strength of parcel wrappers. Provide children with a selection from: newspaper, tissue, brown paper, foil and plastic. Devise and test which is the strongest - try tearing, using weights, making bridges.

Humanities

- Go on a walk around your locality. Identify where post boxes and telephone kiosks are sited and take photographs/drawings of them. Note collection times and instructions on how to use a phone box. Display your findings on a local street map, plotting where the nearest boxes are.
- Show the journey of a particular parcel or letter. Younger children could make a picture sequence - I wrote, I posted, the postman delivered. Older children could make a flow chart showing the process from posting, through sorting to delivery.

- Order your collection of letters into a timeline by looking at the stamps. Use clues like: the change from Kings to Queens; price increases (including before and after decimalisation). Display next to old coins.
- Look at the postmarks on a collection of envelopes. Find out where they were posted. **Display like this:**

- Use pictures, drawings or rubbings of the fronts of post boxes to order into a timeline.

Art and Craft/Design and Technology
- Design and make a class post-box. Think about size of letter opening and how you will get the mail out.
- Design and make a message pad to hang on the wall. How will the pen be attached?
- Position and overlap old envelopes to build up a raised pattern. Use this as a base from which to take rubbings. Display alongside each other.
- Provide a range of pencils with different grades of lead (mostly soft, some hard). Make an outline of a telephone box and fill it in with a range of tones and textures.

- **Make a paper sculpture,** experimenting with the effects of curl, tear, fold, scrunch, wave, screw.

Music
- Make the sound effects of a postman calling. Draw simple picture cue cards showing the postman on his rounds: opening and shutting the gate; walking up the path; post dropping on the mat. Use voice/body sounds or instruments to create the sound effects of these. Encourage children to add their own musical ideas to the story, e.g. knocking at the door; trudging up a snowy path; chased by a dog. Can others guess what is happening?
- Singing addresses. You have the notes E and G on chime bars (or other pitched instrument) to sing and play 'Where do you live?' (G G G E) to each of the children in turn. The children respond by singing their own 'tune' on these two notes, e.g. 'I live in Town Close' (G E E G E). It may help them to say/clap their rhythm before singing it. Leave the two chimes available for the children to get a feel of moving up and down this 'jump' and invent their own tunes.

Further activities from the book
- Make a picture sequence showing the order in which the postman delivered the post. Display in the shape of Post Office vans.
- Make an alternative Jolly Postman book using the same design, e.g. a birthday flap book from Goldilocks to baby bear; the wolf trying to sell double-glazing to the little pig in the brick house; a gift pack of seeds from Jack to the giant.
- Make a bag for the postman to carry the six envelopes he delivered.
- Design a stamp for an imaginary land, like the one 'Giant Bigg' might live in. Talk about and list all the features of the land. Select aspects which best characterise the country, and incorporate these into first and second class stamp designs.
- Choose one of the characters and show their response to receiving the post. Cinderella (or another character) could either tell a friend, write a diary entry, or show her reaction in thought bubbles.
- Make a model village from construction kits, or junk materials. Use the pictures and addresses in the book for clues on planning: where is Horner's Corner sited? Where will you put the signpost pointing towards Banbury Cross - what might be on the other arms?

Dinosaurs

MEG'S EGGS, Helen Nicoll and Jan Pienkowski (Picture Puffin)
Long Neck and Thunderfoot, Helen Piers. **Dinosaur Dreams,** A.Ahlberg/A.Amstutz.
The Village Dinosaur, Phyllis Arkle.

Collections
Dinosaur models in all forms: soft toys, mobiles, inflatables, wooden skeletons. Pictures and books showing present day reptiles, mosses, ferns and climatic conditions then and now.

Starters
Enjoy the challenge of looking through books together and sounding out dinosaur names. Discuss and make a list (on a flip chart, on tape or in note books) of the children's ideas about dinosaurs. Were they just huge, savage monsters or real creatures? Are they still alive? Help the children to decide what else they would like to find out about dinosaurs. Encourage them to check the accuracy of these initial thoughts after research. Talk about 'early earth' ideas (see Humanities). Try to give children first-hand experience of touching fossils and bones (take Plasticine imprints of shells to give an idea of how fossils are formed). Read creation stories to share ideas about how the world might have begun. Visit the Natural History/local museum to look at skeletons and rocks.

English
- Retell a dinosaur story using shadow/stick puppets. Can the children make a sequel or change the ending?
- Play a game of twenty questions. Arrange 5/7 dinosaurs on a felt board (or use toy dinosaurs). Can the children guess, by describing the dinosaur's features, or where it is on the line (first, middle, facing left etc) which one you have chosen?

Tumblosaurus

- Invent your own dinosaurs. Make up a name that fits a particular description. Research the fact that dino=terrible, saurus=lizard, triceratops=three-horned lizard. What would you call a dinosaur who was always falling over?
- Make up a silly sentence about a particular dinosaur. Use the first letter of its name to create a sentence like 'Clever Corythosaurus cooking cakes in Canada'.
- Make up sentences about dinosaurs so that children can sort them into sets of true/false. The children can make up their own true/false sentences, e.g, 'Stegosaurus had bony plates along its back' (true), 'Diplodocus had two spiky thumbs to fight with' (false).
- Make an acrostic about a particular dinosaur's difficult day.

Maths
- Take some model dinosaurs and, without using weights, get the children to put them in order from heaviest to lightest. Check using weights/balances. Record your findings.
- Relate dinosaur measurements to objects and sizes familiar to the children. Take one of the dinosaurs as the centre of a display. Around this, write dinosaur facts and dimensions with child-friendly comparisons, e.g. 'It's —-m long. Two of these dinosaurs would fit along the wall. It's as tall as a bus. It weighs —- kilos, so one dinosaur is the same as twelve of me.'
- Draw outlines of dinosaurs on squared or dotty paper. Colour these in and compare the dinosaurs - whose is the largest? How do we compare them? (See photograph opposite.)
- How many eyes on 5 dinosaurs? 1 dinosaur has four feet - how many on 2/4? Iguanodon had 2 spiky thumbs - how many would 2 have? Show number patterns on pegboards/100 square/number track.
- Play 'race for home'. Use a 100 square as a base board. Compsognathus runs quickly and starts at 0. Diplodocus plods - place counter on 50. Throw a die (or pick up cards) marked 2, 4, 6. Compsognathus moves by doubling the score thrown. Diplodocus moves by halving scores. Who reaches home (100) first? Is it fair? Experiment with different starting positions.

Science

● Think about dinosaurs and camouflage. In a large carton make a landscape which includes trees, swamp area and open ground. Have a collection of simple card dinosaurs with tab stands to place on the landscape. Which dinosaurs are hidden best in different parts of the landscape?

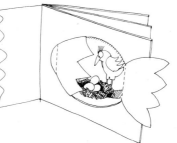

● Look at creatures that lay eggs as dinosaurs did. Which are reptiles? **Make a book which opens up like a cracked egg.** Show what's inside and where it lays its eggs.

● Compare dinosaurs to present day reptiles (crocodile, lizard, turtle). Make simple labelled diagrams to show how they are the same (scaly skin, claws, plant/meat eaters), and different (size, colour, extinct).
● Research dinosaur skeletons. Make a 3D model using art straws, pipe cleaners, rolled paper tubes. Or make a flat skeleton on black paper from cut straws, polystyrene, match sticks.
● Make a dinosaur fact file. Include information like: measurements, food eaten, amazing facts. You could use an IT branch program to identify dinosaurs, or put all the contributions into a class book, giving it a picture index.
● Dinosaurs died out about 65 million years ago. Use information from conservation groups to find out about endangered species. Make an 'action' poster on how to prevent them from becoming extinct.

Humanities

● Try being archaeologists. Dig for your own information in the school grounds. Get the children to chart carefully the different layers in the earth, and any finds.
● Talk to the children about why dinosaurs may have died out. Brainstorm and list their ideas. Compare these with the ideas you can find in books.
● Draw a picture sequence showing what happens to a dinosaur from the time it dies by a lake and becomes fossilised, to the bones being found and reconstructed.
● Talk and find out about 'early earth' and where human beings fit into such a huge time span. Make a giant timeline going right across the classroom showing the development from: rock> seas> plants> sea animals> land animals> dinosaurs> man.

● Cut out dinosaur silhouettes and, on a world map, plot where they have been found (North America, Europe, Africa). What did a map of the world look like during the age of the dinosaurs?

Art and Craft/Design and Technology
● Make dinosaur shapes by printing with hands. Try out different effects - print with full/flat hand, side, finger tips/ball, side of fingers, rolling movements.
● Make sewn, stuffed dinosaurs. The fabric and materials used could reflect the characteristics of actual dinosaurs - scales, smooth/pitted skin etc. Display on a landscape made from boxes arranged in different heights and draped with fabric. Show dinosaurs of land, sea and air.
● Make life-size dinosaurs using chalks. What different textures can you create using the chalk on its side, using the tip, or smudging?
● Make dinosaur models with moving parts - Tyrannosaurus with snapping jaws, Ankylosaurus with a club tail that swings, Compsognathus with quick-moving legs.

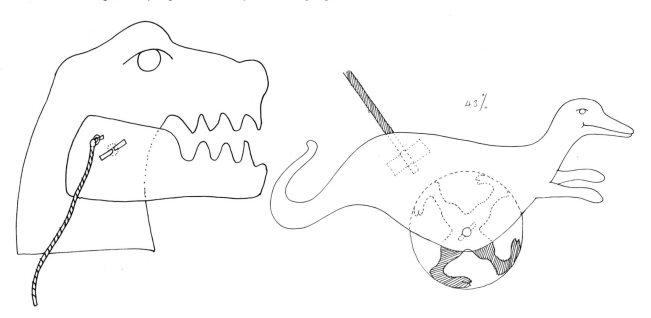

Music
● Match instruments to the different dinosaurs: slow heavy Diplodocus (drum, tambour); Stegosaurus with rattling, bony plates (tambourine/wood blocks); snapping jaws of Tyrannosaurus (clappers, symbols). Retell a dinosaur story, leaving space for groups to play their chosen instruments whenever their dinosaur's name is mentioned. Tape and evaluate the performance. Try out different instruments and combinations. Build up other sound effects in a similar way.
● Learn the song 'Pre-historic Animal Brigade' *(Okki-Tokki-Unga,* A & C Black). Add dance movements suggested by the words - beak clacking, teeth snapping, feet stomping.

Further activities from the book
● Use instruments to show a sequence of the dinosaurs emerging from the eggs. Look at words like 'tap, tap' (short, sharp sounds), 'creak, crack' (long, drawn-out sounds). What do the dinosaurs do when they finally come out - snap, scurry, tumble about? How can these movements be represented by instruments?
● Take some of the sound words like: plink, plonk, plunk, or creak, crack. Put words that begin with the same blend in a cauldron. Use these to invent your own spell to make Tyrannosaurus Rex less fierce.
● Take a toy dinosaur and make a wheeled model to move it from one place to another - a trolley, wheelbarrow or buggy.
● Look at how the egg cups are arranged in a triangular pattern on the table. How many different place settings can you make? Add another egg cup for a surprise guest. How many place settings can you make now?
● Diplodocus grew very fast. Chart how you've grown (weight, height) since you were born. Predict how much you think you'll grow in another year/six years.

Air, Wind and Flight

Make a frieze showing the girl's flight in *Up and Up*

UP AND UP, Shirley Hughes (Red Fox)
The Wind Blew, Pat Hutchin. **Robert the Pilot,** Philippe Dupasquier. **Ursula Ballooning,** Sheila Lavelle.
Mr. Potter's Pigeon, Patrick Kinmouth/Reg Cartwright.

Collections
Toy windmills, balloons, hand fans, mobiles, toy parachutes. Vacuum cleaner, electrical fan. Models and pictures of old and new flying machines. Aerial photographs of the school/local environment, and associated maps, models or ground-level photographs.

Starters
Brainstorm the children's ideas about what wind is and where it comes from. Go outside for clues: what can they see, feel and hear? List the things being moved by air: ruffled clothing/hair, litter blowing around, clouds scudding, trees rustling. Let the children hold a piece of stiff card in front of them and notice what happens when they run into, or with, the wind. Look at picture symbols on the Beaufort scale and talk about the differences between: breeze, strong winds, gale, hurricane. Display vocabulary (blow, whistle, hum, drone etc) as a puff of wind scattering the words.

English
● Talk about fantastical ways of flying: on a broomstick, giant sycamore seed, the back of a dragon, tied to a bunch of balloons. Put ideas into an 'If I Could Fly' book.
● Make a simple model of a town/landscape (from, e.g., Duplo/farm set). Give directions as a flight controller to a Red Arrows pilot: over the steeple, between the roofs, around the hill. The 'pilot' follows this path with a toy plane. Write up the flight path in a loopy jet trail form.
● Make a list of small, light items to put into a flight bag to keep yourself amused.
● Have a simplified balloon debate. Get children to wear a hat/label showing themselves as an important person in school (cook, secretary, head teacher, child). Each one gives a sentence saying why they are useful and should not be thrown out of the balloon. You could go on to display the given reasons as pictures and speech bubbles.

● Write a letter to grandma telling her that, as first prize in a competition, you have won a ride in a hot air balloon; or, write as the promoters to the lucky winner.

Maths

● Sort a collection of 'flying pictures' or models into: birds, insects, seeds, machines, other (kite, parachute, Super Ted).
● How much does a balloon weigh flat/inflated? What balances the inflated balloon? Try bottle tops, polystyrene pieces, dried pulses or corks. Can you find just one object to balance the balloon?

● Pop the balloons game.
Pop all the balloons to help the girl land safely. Throw dice and pop the balloons by covering the number with a counter. According to ability, use the dice to: match the number; find the sum/difference; multiply.

● Make kite shapes on pin boards (or draw on dotty paper). Can you make kites with 1,2,3,4 pins inside?
● Use Velcro or rubber suction darts and scoreboards to practise number bonds.
● Draw a rocket, plane or windmill shape on squared paper. Give it to a friend to copy or describe the co-ordinates of squares to make one exactly the same. Younger children can use Polydron, Link bricks or solid shapes.

Science

● Predict and then test how objects fall through the air: feather, seed, crisp bag, tissue, cork. Do they all float and fall in the same way?

● **Make spirals or spinners to hang around the class** (over warm air or draughts). Which move slowly/quickly, and why?

● Blow some bubbles - which surfaces will they land/burst on? Try different shaped holders (tubes, squeezy bottles, wire frames). Predict which shaped bubble you'll get.
● Explore the properties of balloons: stretchiness, transparency, noises. Inflate a balloon and let it go. Record the directions it travels - any patterns? Can they be controlled/directed in any way?
● Find out how many different ways you can move a paper aeroplane along the ground, using air power. Try flapping a piece of paper, blowing through a straw, making a fan. Encourage the children to be as inventive as possible. Chart the results.
● Think about air pollution. Choose different places to hang up pieces of filter paper covered with Vaseline. Predict, then record, any changes.

Humanities

● On a world map, show a flight the children have, or would like to make, to another part of the world. Place a coloured strip on the map from home to the chosen country. Identify the areas of sea and land passed over during the flight. Record this information as postcards to display around the map.
● Look at local airports. Find out about destinations of outgoing flights, and where incoming flights originated. Display as a simple diagram with the airport in the centre. Add incoming/outgoing arrows labelling names of countries/regions.

- Describe scenes as from a bird's-eye view. Can the children describe part of the school or locality (shopping centre, swimming pool, etc.) so that others can guess where they might be hovering in a helicopter?
- Find out about famous flight stories, e.g. Montgolfier brothers, Amy Johnson, Neil Armstrong. Retell these stories, add pictures and present as an Early Flight book.

Art and Craft/Design and Technology
- Create vapour trails, or the whirls/swirls of a windy day, using combs, scrapers and thick paint. Use as a background for silhouette shapes of flying craft.
- Make bubble prints for a frieze of hot air balloons and mount on chalked 'cloudscapes'.
- Use construction toys to design and make an aircraft to carry 6 Lego people, or a cargo of 4 bricks.
- Use junk materials to make a mobile/hanging display of real or fantastical forms of flight (see English).
- Make a draught excluder for a bedroom. Think about where it will be placed, length, shape, materials, stuffing and decoration (e.g. dragon, hot dog).
- Design a stand-up sign which uses wind to make it turn - such as may be seen outside an airport or garage. Think about how it is shaped to catch the wind, and how to make it stable.

Music
- Make windy sounds with voices. Take the children's ideas and draw/write each sound on a card. You may want to show pitch (high/low) or volume.

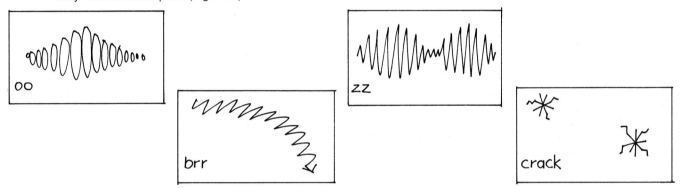

Put the cards in a sequence and sing them in order from left to right. Change the order and include some repeats.
- Explore the sounds made by 'wind instruments'. Blow across the tops of bottles (filled with different amounts of water). Use swanee whistles, recorder, kazoo, whistles, ocarina, melodica/triola, or pinch the neck of an inflated balloon. Listen to Rimsky-Korsakov's 'Flight of the Bumble Bee'. Make up your own compositions, e.g. flight of the kite, jet or humming bird.

Further activities from the book
- In pairs, retell the 'Up and Up' story (or parts of it) through the pictures. Look carefully at facial expressions and interesting detail (fried eggs falling, plates smashing). Use puppets and/or sound effects to help.
- Use the opening spread of the bird's-eye view of the town as a clue spotter. Look at the kinds of old and new buildings and the materials used to build them. What games and leisure activities are shown? What time of year/day is it?
- Make up a cumulative game based on the people waiting at the bus stop. In a circle, the children could add another character. Can they get them in the right sequence and remember them all?
- What makes the children rush to the window in school? Make a card window frame. On a large strip of card, stick a series of pictures showing surprises like the fire engine, snow, giant's feet. Slide the card from left to right behind the frame to view the scene from the window.
- Focus on a particular frame or sequence, add speech/thought bubbles to interesting developments, e.g. the surprised parents or the little girl who might be thinking, 'So that's what people look like upside down.'
- Trace part of the flying route taken by the girl in *Up and Up*. Ask the children to draw a map for her future use. Which obstacles might prove hazardous (low buildings, trees, church spires, chimneys)?

Farming

KATIE MORAG AND THE TWO GRANDMOTHERS, M. Hedderwick (Collins Picture Lions)
Rosie's Walk, Pat Hutchins. *Early Morning in the Barn,* Nancy Tafuri. *Farmer Duck,* Martin Waddell.
Charlotte's Web, E.B.White.

Collections

Toy farm animals, buildings and machines. Posters and flyers promoting farm machinery, farming publications. Woollen jumpers, untreated sheep's wool, sheepskin rugs and clothing, loom/spinning wheel. Dairy product labels and wrappers. Selection of breads: French, pitta, chapatti, rolls, wholemeal etc. Cereal and flour packets.

Starters

Be sensitive about vegetarian diets, allergic reactions and religions which forbid certain foods. Stress the importance of washing hands after handling food wrappers. Talk about and make a picture bank of farming activities the children may already know about. Brainstorm words associated with farming (livestock, crops, equipment) and use as the beginnings of a thematic list. What sorts of things can the children recall from books, TV, pictures, visits? Establish the idea that a farm is a home and an industry. Discuss different types of farms: arable, sheep, mixed, fruit, etc. Chart the similarities/differences between rural farms, city farms, small holdings, allotments. Visit a farm or a farm shop, if possible, and invite farming personnel to talk to the children about their jobs.

English/Role Play

- Make a set of word and picture cards of animal family groups (bull, cow, calf, etc). Use these for: sorting and setting into families, playing Snap, Pelmanism, Happy Families, Sound Lotto, Twenty Questions.
- Make a poster about one aspect of the Country Code, e.g. close gates behind you; take your litter home. Arrange these posters as part of a farmers' display stand in a marquee at an agricultural show. (See photograph opposite.)
- Find out about children's classes in agricultural shows (making fruit/vegetable necklaces, potato/parsnip creatures; painting/collage of farm scenes and animals etc). Set up your play area as a children's marquee. Make certificates, rosettes, and exhibit labels. Children display all their 'competition entries' and role play: hot (disgruntled, enthusiastic) visitors, judges, caterers etc.
- Using imaginary characters, e.g. Farmer Bright and Farmer Glum, explore the advantages and disadvantages of a farmer's life. Choose one aspect, e.g. getting up early. Children take on the role of either farmer and express how they feel about it, e.g. 'I love hearing the dawn chorus' (Farmer Bright) and 'I wish I was still in bed, it's cold and wet' (Farmer Glum). These can be put into pairs of cartoon frames and compiled as a class book or frieze.
- Discuss how you should behave near animals/machinery. You could put the ideas into a hand-out that a farmer might send to schools thinking of visiting them.
- A farm visit is offered as 'first prize' in a competition. Write or draw your entry listing five things you would most like to see/do there.

Maths

- Compare the capacity of different milk containers: bottles, card cartons, plastic bag. How can you find out which holds the most?
- Use cereal boxes to: order by size (height, depth, area); set by type of grain used and chart popularity. Look at solid shapes and nets of the boxes. Compare prices and 'bargain buys' - is an economy size cheaper than two smaller ones?
- Do a milk survey: work out how much milk is taken by the children's families in a day/week/month. Display using full and half bottle shapes. Relate the findings to how much milk a cow produces each day.

- Use a model farm layout. Count, sort and classify types of animals (number of feet, size, colours, walk/fly/swim). Investigate number problems (computing numbers of animals in different fields; how many legs/tails/eyes on 1,2,3...cows; share a number of sheep equally between pens). **Explore shape: investigate open/closed shapes for pens,** look at plane shapes of enclosures, parallel and diagonal lines on gates, horizontal rails, vertical posts and right angles on fencing. (See line drawings at left.)

Make a 'country code' poster (see English section)

● A farmer has 18 metres of fencing. Make pens with different perimeters. Which is the largest area possible?

Science
● In picture sequence form, show how a jumper is made - from the sheep shearing to the finished product. You can do the same for dairy produce - from cow to yoghurt, cheese or a bottle of milk, and for grain - from harvest to the breakfast cereal or bread.
● Investigate by-products from animals and grain. Collect wrappers, labels, and magazine pictures associated with cows: cheeses, yoghurts, ice cream, skins, garments etc. (Display by having the animal in the centre and the by-products around the outside showing which parts have been used.) For grain, collect: cereal wrappers, flour, crispbread, malt drinks etc.
● Make a 'spotter's guide to farm animals'. The whole class, small groups or individuals, find out about various animals and record their findings on cards to build into a reference bank. Suggested headings: name of animal; description (size/colour/features); food eaten; tracks; by-products; interesting facts (heaviest/largest example recorded etc).
● Grow wheat or barley seeds. Experiment with different soils (loam, clay, sandy) and adding fertilisers.
● Grind wheat seeds between a range of materials: wooden spoons, hammer, large/small stones, soft/hard wood. Which work best?

Humanities
● Look at/discuss pictures of animal housing used on farms. Design, draw or paint a range of farm buildings: machinery stores, grain or fodder stores, dairy.
● Do a town survey looking for clues linking the community with farms past and present: the market place or corn exchange; street names, e.g. The Shambles, Weavers Way, Barley Row. Take photographs or drawings and display on a town map.
● Find out about the farming year for a sheep, dairy or grain farmer. How are their lives affected by different weather conditions? Look at seasonal differences in farming activities: clothing worn, whether the animals are outside or in. Display on a wheel with a hand moving through the seasons.

● Collect and look at labels for country of origin. Which crops can be grown in Britain? Which ones can't (rice, sugar cane, cocoa, coffee)? Find out more about the relationship between crops and climate. You could display your findings like this:

● Find out about tools and machinery used on farms today. Look at the continued use of hand tools (spades, hoes, rakes) and animal power. How has the invention of the tractor and combine harvester changed things? Display the information in a tractor-shaped picture book.

Art and Craft/Design and Technology
● Make field landscapes. Use ribbed fabrics such as cord or hessian for field textures and natural materials like grains, wood shavings, string, sheep or horse hair.
● Make farm animals with moving parts - a duck with flapping wings, or a nodding cow's head.

● Use a simple card loom to weave with wools.

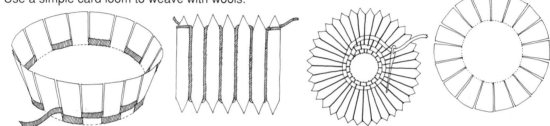

● Design a jumper on squared paper. Colour in a knitting motif with a farming theme for the front of the jumper.
● Design a scarecrow for a farmer's field showing how sounds or movement scare off the birds.

Music
● Help the children to make a sound cassette to use in class or, for a younger class, include: nursery rhymes (Little Bo Peep, Baa Baa Black Sheep) and some cumulative songs ('Old MacDonald' or 'Buttercup Farm', from *Silly Aunt Sally,* Ward Lock Educational). Make a sound spot game: record farm animal noises separately, leaving space in between each sound. Then try taping two noises at the same time - can the children identify/distinguish between the cow and the horse? Record 'The Dingle Dangle Scarecrow' to use as an action song, and make up some simple jangly scarecrow music to dance to between verses.

Further activities from the book
● Look closely at the inside cover picture of the Isle of Struay and make a model of its layout.
● Make card dolls representing Grannie Island and Granma Mainland. Draw and cut out paper clothing with tabs. Dress the dolls in clothes suitable for messy farm jobs and smart town wear.
● Based on the beautifying products favoured by Granma Mainland, collect containers and write labels showing what various items are used for: moisturiser, hair spray, perfume etc.
● Look at how Katie and Grannie washed the sheep. Investigate ways of removing dirt from hands/fabric. Try: cold water; cold water and soap; warm water; warm water and soap.
● Consider all the sounds made at the show: the hustle and bustle of people talking, shouting, animals, machines, music for dancing, clinking of cutlery. Use the sound words to make a class poem.
● Make preparations for your own 'village show'. Use Katie Morag to help plan what's to be included. You could make a list of exhibition stands, sites, competitions, entrance fees etc. Make a programme of events and advertise the show.

Sizes

Things which are **thinner** than Stanley.

- a pancake
- a button
- an envelope
- a photograph
- a leaf
- a watch strap
- a tissue
- a stamp

- a dictionary
- a door
- a sandwich box
- a box of chocolates
- a cake
- a tennis ball
- a table
- a videocassette

Can you think of more things?

Things which are **thicker** than Stanley.

FLAT STANLEY, Jeff Brown (Mammoth)
Titch, Pat Hutchins. *Jim and the Beanstalk,* Raymond Briggs.
The Shrinking of Treehorn, Florence Parry Heide. *The Indian in the Cupboard,* Lynne Reid Banks.

Collections

Large and small pairs of natural and man-made objects: stones, toys, plants, musical instruments, books. Scale models, a doll's house, Russian dolls, stacking toys, nesting trays.

Starters

Use your collection for ordering by size and to focus on comparative language - smaller/taller/wider than. Display sizes vocabulary (including the colloquial - wee, tinsy etc) on pairs of tiny and big outlines of, e.g. people, buildings, flowers. Ask the children to recall the names of giants and little folk from stories and myths. Talk about how the children themselves have changed over time - growth and the sorts of things they can do now that they couldn't manage when smaller (see Humanities). Try to arrange a visit to a model village, huge buildings or massive landmarks.

English

● Brainstorm synonyms for large and small: great, huge, gigantic, enormous, minute, microscopic, petite. The children can use these to describe their own fantasy characters, e.g. Giant Huge has a colossal body, great big feet, enormous teeth. Try the same for tiny characters. Illustrate the descriptions and collect into giant and miniature books.

● **Make up sentences about relative sizes,** e.g. 'A cat is huge next to a mouse, but is small next to a giraffe.'

A cat is huge next to a mouse, but...

It is small next to a giraffe!

17

- Write 'tall stories'- give them a magical feel, about people and objects that might grow and shrink. Or write stories that will never be believed on long, thin paper.
- Make sentences that grow. Start with a short sentence, e.g. 'Kieron sat on a tractor'. Children take turns to add interesting words to the sentence - 'Kieron sat on a bright, new, shiny, red, tractor'. This approach is easily adapted to a poem format: each line has one more word - tree, tall tree, tall leafy tree...
- Make a really useful 'Pocket Guide' or match box collection for a baby elf. What could a stamp, a cork, a piece of string be used for?
- Use a dictionary to find words with more than eight letters. Some children could give picture definitions.
- Make a longer word (as in the game of Scrabble). Children take turns to add a letter anywhere in the word to make a new one, e.g. at - pat - path - patch.

Maths

- Ordering: find a range of different sized circles and draw round them (junk lids and containers, bin, card shapes, counters). Cut out and decorate, then order by size. Try the same with other shapes. **String them together to display.**

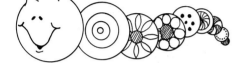

- Make a comparatives display. Take one object in different lengths (pencil, tube, paint brush) and label: long, longer, longest. Do the same for other measurements - width and thickness.
- Match different lengths of straws to a range of containers - are the straws long enough to reach over the rim?
- What do big numbers look like? Can the children estimate 100 straws, cubes, coins, Duplo/house bricks, chairs, children, grains of sugar? Test out their ideas - any surprises? Choose a container: estimate, then look at the space some of these take up.
- Use cards numbered 0 - 9. Pick up two cards and order them to make the biggest/smallest number (92, 29). Try with three cards.
- Make a data bank of personal measurements. Use it to find out if the tallest people have: the biggest shoe sizes, widest hand span, can jump the furthest.
- Play giants: whatever the children do, the giant does it x2 (x5, x10), e.g. I ate 2 sausages, 1 egg, 2 slices of bread - what does the giant have? Make other comparisons: I drink 2 litres, jump 1.5 metres, sleep for 7 hours. Tricky ones include: size of shoes, blanket, toy box. Play it in reverse - halve everything for tiny people.

Science

- Soak some dried peas in water. Predict and then observe the changes. Does anything else change size when left in water? Test out the children's ideas.
- Make a 'little and large' animal book. Illustrate animals and their young. Or, research big and small pairs, e.g. the longest/shortest snake; the largest/smallest dinosaur.
- Do all tiny seeds grow into tiny plants (and the reverse)? Predict and then plant seeds to find out. Older children can research heights, looking at seed packets and catalogues, and chart their findings - any surprises?
- Try stretching different materials: loose-weave fabric, balloon, plastic, crêpe paper. Which changes size the most (sideways, top to bottom, bias)? Can any materials be scrunched up to make them smaller? Try wood, metal, clay, cling film, aluminium foil, tissue, bread.
- Make huge/tiny shadows. Use a slide projector/lamp to cast shadows on the wall. What has to be done to the objects/light source to make shadows grow and shrink? How can their shapes be changed? Cut out head-shaped silhouettes to make your own giants.

Humanities

- Make a 'How we've grown' display. Talk to the children about how much they've grown and changed since they were babies (they might bring in family photographs). Compare clothing of the baby, toddler, child, adult (shoes, trousers, gloves). Use old clothing or silhouette shapes to order by size as part of the display.

- Make a local Spotter's Guide including features like: the longest road, oldest building, biggest shop.
- Make picture sequences showing geographical features that grow in size or get smaller, e.g. spring-stream-river-sea; cliff-boulder-rocks-pebbles-sand grains.
- Try drawing giant's eye views (like bird's eye) of items on your display table. Try an ant's eye view. Display the drawings next to the objects.

Art and Craft/Design and Technology

- Design things that change size.

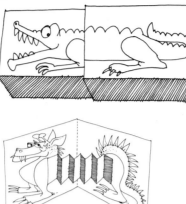

- Model a giant's meal: the plate, cutlery, a huge plate of salad.
- Take some 30cm lengths of string, ribbon or laces. **Attach them all at one point and pull them around to change size and shape.**

- Make your own giant world by juxtaposing magazine pictures, e.g. a tiny person next to a huge cat licking its lips; a tiny dog sitting on the rim of an enormous plate.
- Microscopic art: Use magnifiers to look at fine detail and patterns in crystals, skeleton leaves, wood, fabric, seed heads. Select appropriate drawing tools and draw only what you see.
- Make some doll's house furniture, just the right size for a soft toy/Lego person.
- List all the things which would be difficult if you were only half your size. Design and make something to help, e.g. reach and ring a door bell; press buttons in a telephone kiosk; depress a door lever.

Music

- In groups of three, make 'Three Bears' sounds. Daddy Bear makes a body/voice sound. Mummy Bear makes the same sound a little quieter, and Baby Bear as quietly as possible. Choose another sound and repeat. Try starting with baby and making the sounds grow.
- Find out which instruments can make long, ringing sounds. Can you make a long sound shorter?
- Take three different chime bars: play them and order by pitch (high-low). Try with different sized triangles and glockenspiel bars. Can the children make any link between sounds and sizes?
- In pairs, take an instrument and make the smallest (softest, shortest) sound you can. See if a friend can make their smallest sound in a different way.

Further activities from the book

- Think up similes about being flat (Stanley is 'as flat as a pancake'). Can the children make their lettering complement the theme by being long and thin?
- Set up your own museum of art. Collect prints, postcards, magazine pictures. Make picture frames; exhibit cards; make a catalogue and price tags. Add the children's own paintings to the museum.
- Dress up as someone in a famous painting (like Stanley's disguise) and sit for your own portrait.
- Can the children use outlines of themselves to make and fly a Flat Stanley type kite?
- Record, in words or pictures, extracts of Stanley's 'after I got flattened' diary. Include the sequence of major events, e.g. I get measured; I get dangled down a drain; I get air-mailed to California ...
- **How many squares are needed to frame a square picture?** Try framing larger pictures.
- Display the pros and cons of being flat like Stanley: sliding under doors, retrieving things from inaccessible places, exciting hiding places, falling down open staircases, being knocked over when someone sneezes, sitting in front of the French horns during a concert...

Bicycles and Wheels

JULIAN'S GLORIOUS SUMMER, Ann Cameron (Gollancz)
Mrs. Armitage on Wheels, Quentin Blake. **Stanley Bagshaw and the Fourteen Foot Wheel,** Bob Wilson.
Wheels, Shirley Hughes.

Collections

A bicycle labelled to show pedals, wheels, saddle, pump etc. Display the Green Cross Code, RoSPA posters and other aspects of safety: cycling proficiency, helmets, luminous strips, reflectors. A selection of pictures and artefacts showing a range of wheeled objects (not all transport): buggy, shopping trolley, skate board, tractor, water/wind mills, fairground wheels.

Starters

What sorts of things do the children know about that use wheels? Brainstorm ideas and help them to sort the collection of pictures and objects, e.g. those which go on the road (car, lorry, van, bicycle) and those which don't (goods trains). Discuss which forms of transport the children have used themselves - where did they go and who drives? Count wheels on different objects/vehicles, and look at a range of shapes, sizes, colours and tread patterns (from bald to caterpillar). Find out how wheels are attached - what are axles for? Look carefully at what happens when wheels turn. Collect and display wheelie words (see English).

English

- Brainstorm wheelie words to make a vocabulary bank. Have a wheel shape, and in between the spokes display children's ideas of movement words (roll, spin, revolve etc). Try other wheel banks: parts of a bicycle; bi-words (biplane, bilingual); maths words (circle, circumference).
- Make and decorate a menu card for a party with a wheelie theme. All food must be circular, e.g. Swiss roll, egg rolls, slices of cucumber.
- Make up an 'Old Bike, New Bike' poem, either individually or as a class. Compare and contrast the old and the new, thinking about describing parts of the bike, e.g. the shiny paint, springy saddle, rattling pedals, bent rusty spokes.
- Circle story: sitting in a circle, children take turns making contributions to a class story. Have a selection of wheeled pictures and objects - roller boots, steam roller (see Collections). At intervals, a child selects one of these to introduce into the story. Give a traditional tale character a bicycle, e.g. the wood cutter comes to Red Riding Hood's rescue on a bone shaker; substitute the knight's white charger for a BMX. Draw/write the new version of the tale.
- Make some phonic wheels.

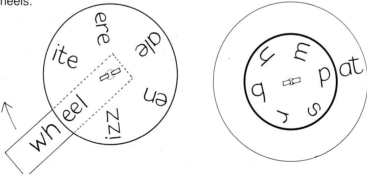

- Make a check list of all the information that can be found on a book's dust cover: title, author, illustrator, publisher, blurb/synopsis, ISBN number. Choose a bicycle/wheels book and fill in the check list.

Maths

- Find out which solid shapes roll down a gentle slope. Do they all roll in the same way? What pathways do they make - straight lines, curves, clockwise, anti-clockwise?
- Use a trundle wheel to measure the hall, corridor, playground, pathways. How else can big distances be measured?
- Make a picture graph/pie chart showing how children travel to school: wheels or not wheels?

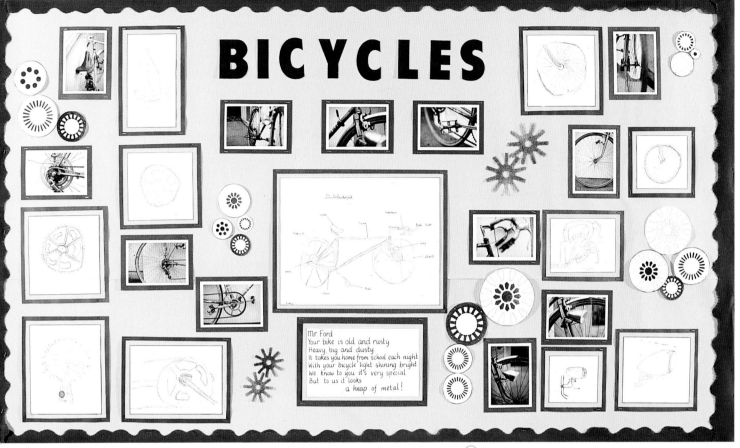

- Calculator wheel

  Start on the hub, and put that number on the calculator display. Move along spokes/wheel rim to another circled number by making the display show that number, e.g. from hub to 6, show 10-4 =6.

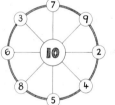

- Investigate how far a bicycle wheel travels as it makes a complete turn (keep a marker on the wheel, match to a mark on the floor). Try different sized wheels, hoops, circular trays - which go furthest?
- On squared paper, draw a 5 by 5 parking space (1 square = 1 car). Make this model with Link bricks, build up levels on top as a multi-storey car park. How many cars can fit on 2/3/4 levels? Record the pattern (change the numbers to suit ability).
- Record letters showing the year of registration on number plates. What is the year of the vehicle? Which are the oldest/newest? Any the same age as the children? Any other observations?

Science

- Investigate how vehicles travel over different surfaces. Make a gentle slope covered with lino, carpet, plastic sheeting, wood - wet/dry. Test the children's predictions - how far/easily does the wheel travel?
- Move a box, brick or other heavy load. Try pulling, using rollers (dowelling, card tubes, pencils) or a wheeled base. Which is the easiest/most difficult?
- Which shapes are best for wheels? Test by trying pairs of card triangles, squares and circles on an axle. How do they move? Which roll easily and what happens if axles are not in the middle of the wheels?
- Make a close observational drawing of a bicycle. Write simple, explanatory labels for major design features, e.g. shape of frame, why wheels are round, how gears, lamps and reflectors work. (See photograph.)
- What do we know about car pollution? Why is a bicycle called 'clean transport'? Talk about when the children use bicycles and cars. When is it impossible to use a cycle? Choose a 'green idea' and make a poster for motorists, e.g. unleaded petrol, sharing rides to work/school.

Humanities

- Set up a model of a road layout and explore: what sorts of things go on the road; why are roads often straight; why do we need traffic lights and crossing places? Use as a basis for practising road safety, for cyclists or pedestrians. Outside, you could make a large route for bikes and wheeled toys.
- Go on a local walk to find out about transport facilities: bus stops, parking meters, road signs, single/multi-storey car parks, taxi ranks. Take photographs/drawings. Why are 'No Parking' zones sited in particular places? Display your findings on a simple map, or labelled model.
- Look at early bicycles and make cartoons of bone shakers, penny farthings, hobby horses. What would it be like to ride these - comfortable, wobbly, exciting? Show in bubbles what the riders might be saying, e.g. 'There's a good view up here', or, 'My bottom hurts!'
- Talk about where the children ride their bicycles. Plan a safe route for a bicycle rally around your locality.

Art and Craft/Design and Technology

- Weaving wheels: make wheels from card or florist's wire (or use bicycle wheels, plastic hoops - make warp threads for spokes). Weave wool, fabric strips and scrap materials (string, raffia, ribbons) in and out of the spokes. Assemble as a display of 'crazy bikes'.
- Make concentric circle tie-dye (use string, buttons, pebbles etc. as markers). Highlight the circular patterns by embroidering/couching threads all round the circles.
- Use construction or junk materials to make: a scooter with 2/3 wheels for a soft toy; or a wheeled barrow big enough for a child to use.
- Draw and label a design for a really zany cycle (Heath Robinson style), for a story book character, e.g. the sneaky wolf who wants a camouflaged bike to take him, his swag bag and disguises, quietly through the woods.

Music

- Help the children to watch for eye-contact signals: sit in a circle and give everyone an instrument. Begin playing a steady rhythm yourself and then look hard at a particular child who starts playing along. That child then 'passes' the signal on to another person in the same way (strong eye contact only). Continue like this until everyone's playing in a circle. Do this in reverse to stop the roll.
- Play and sing circle dances and games. Learn the dances 'Zum gali gali', 'The Whiting' (*The Music Box Song Book* - BBC).
- There is a wonderful selection of singing rounds in *Flying a Round* (A & C Black).

Further activities from the book

- Talk about how Julian felt when he got his new bike. Draw on the children's experience and make a picture and caption sequence for: my first ride, my new bike, thrills and spills. Display on wheel shapes 'rolling' around the frieze.
- Recount some of the 'not quite true' things Julian said. Discuss with the children the times when they've done the same, and what happened. They could go on to draw pairs of pictures with speech bubbles - one showing what was said, the other showing the consequences.
- Print interesting road-way patterns, for Julian to ride along. Use circular or wheel-shaped printers (old cotton reels, plastic wheels, washers, cogs, pencil ends etc).

- **Make your own boomerang wishes** (following Julian's explanation) say the opposite of what you really want. Display like this:

- Make a list of the jobs Julian had to do around the house. What jobs have to be done in your home and who does them? Sort these jobs into: jobs I always do; jobs I sometimes do; those I never do.
- How many complete bikes can you make from 5 saddles, 6 handle bars, 7 frames, 10 pedals, 6 chains, 8 wheels? What's left over?

Cold, Snow and Ice

Make up some wintry similes. Display them on icicle and snowflake shapes and hang them on the silhouette of a winter tree

THE SNOWY DAY, Ezra Jack Keats (Picture Puffin)
The Snowman, Raymond Briggs. *The Snowgirl,* Geraldine Kaye.
The Snow Queen, Hans Christian Andersen. *The Magic Mill,* Joanna Troughton.

Collections

Winter clothes: woolly hats, scarves, gloves, padded jackets, fur-lined boots. Hot water bottles, warming pans, bed socks. Pictures of winter resorts and snowy scenes. Sledge, ice skates, toboggan, skis (pictures or actual objects). Newspaper cuttings of blizzard conditions. Insulating materials: picnic cool box, pipe lagging.

Starters

Think about winter as a season - start a photographic record of seasons, e.g. how does a tree or local park change? What clues about cold weather can the children spot from wintry pictures (frosty puddles, bare trees, icicles, clothing, snowdrops)? Brainstorm and record where else the children have seen ice (fishmonger, freezer, in drinks). Discuss how we keep warm in cold weather: warm clothes, hot food, running around, heaters. On a snowy day, take the children outside for a closer look. What is snow? Why isn't it rain? Observe how snow changes landscape outlines. Put observations into a diary entry for the day - 'What I saw/heard/did'.

English

● Draw a pictorial flow chart, or use a computer, to give step-by-step instructions on how to build a snowman.
● Make a leaflet offering your services to help senior citizens in cold weather. Say what you can do (clear paths, go shopping, carry the coal); times available; contact address/phone number.
● Add your own headlines and/or captions to newspaper clippings and photographs of blizzard conditions.

Maths

● Use pairs of mittens/socks to: match; make repeating patterns (long/short, left/right); count in twos; practise rotation ($1/4$, $1/2$, full turns); reflection.

● **Make snowflakes**

Cut out 3 square and 2 triangular notches. Predict how many squares and triangles the opened snowflake will have and chart the findings. Take made snowflakes, cut each in half along a line of symmetry and use as a matching game. Use mirrors to help find the missing halves.

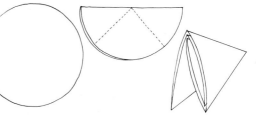

● In your wardrobe you have: 2 hats - red and blue; 2 scarves - yellow and orange; 2 pairs of wellies - green and black. How many days can you go out in the snow wearing different outfits?

● Take strips of card of equal width and cut them into various lengths of 'stripy scarf'.

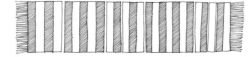

In pairs, take turns to toss a counter marked 'odd' on one side and 'even' on the other. Throw counter. If it shows 'odd' take a piece of card with an odd number of stripes. Do the same for 'even'. Place cards end to end to make a long scarf. Who has the longest scarf at the end of the game?

● To find out what the local ice cream seller needs to stock up on, make a survey of the children's favourite flavours and types.

● Make a scarf 1m long from a sheet of newspaper. How can you make the scarf 50cm/2m long?

Science

● What kinds of weather do the children expect in winter (fog, frost, hail, snow)? Test out their predictions by keeping a pictorial chart showing the weather for each day.

● Which fabrics keep us warmest? Wrap different materials around empty drinks cans (wool, cotton, newspaper, fur). Leave one can uncovered. Fill each can with hot water. Feel/take temperature at intervals. Which stays warmest for longest?

● Make ice lollies, putting sticks in different shaped containers (cube tray, ice cream carton, plastic egg boxes, yoghurt pots, plastic bag). Remove from containers and record the changes carefully. How do the frozen shapes match the original containers?

● Chart how quickly ice cubes melt. Put them in different positions - indoors, outside, near a radiator, in fridge/freezer.

● Look at the effect of ice in drinks. Measure liquid level before/after, temperature change, dilution in squash.

● Introduce children to thermometers. Test the temperature in parts of the room/outside. Where is the coldest place? Cut out thermometers and colour them showing various temperatures.

● Research the different ways of keeping warm and dry indoors - central heating, thick curtains, double glazing etc. Make charts to show which are used in school and which are used in the home. Compare and discuss reasons for the similarities and differences.

● Find out what happens to animals in winter. Display your findings either as a book or wall frieze showing: hibernation, migration and other adaptations, e.g. growing thicker coats.

Humanities

● Use newspaper and television forecasts, local weather bureaux and relatives, to find out what is happening in other parts of the country/world when it's snowing where you are.

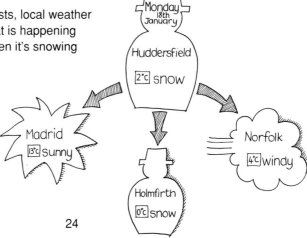

- Look closely at cold weather pictures from Christmas cards, prints of winter scenes by famous artists, photographs of the children's relations, for clues into how people kept warm in the past. Talk about similarities and differences between then and now. Choose one of the pictures and make your own present day 'keeping warm' scene in the same style.
- Which countries have regular snow and what preparations are made to deal with it? Look at adaptations to transport, houses, clothes. Find/draw and label pictures showing adaptations (chains on car wheels, plough in front of train, steep roofs etc).

Art and Craft/Design and Technology
- Make a frieze of winter games and sports. Talk about games the children play in the snow and look for others in pictures and books.
- Make a snow storm scene. Put model figures (snowmen, houses, trees etc) into a screw-top jar. Fill the jar with water and 'snow' - use desiccated coconut, crumbled polystyrene, finely cut silver foil pieces, shredded candle wax. Shake the jar.
- Make snow crystal patterns. Use lace, sequins, tinsel, lurex threads, glitter, paper clips, buttons, rice and doilies.
- Design a snow plough - make a digger front to plough a pathway through the sand tray.
- Make snow and ice sculptures out of junk materials. Try shiny effects using salt, glitter, bottle tops, scrunched foil, polystyrene. Cover boxes with white/metallic papers, paint and crayons. Put together into an Antarctic scene.
- Decorate the word 'COLD' and 'SNOW'

- Make a sledge or toboggan from junk materials or construction toys. Think about type of runner and seating position. Make a slope for it to run down.

Music and Movement
- Play extracts from the sound track of 'The Snowman', Raymond Briggs (music by Howard Blake), and interpret the music through actions. Try falling snowflakes: light, floaty, curling and swirling movements. Snowman shapes: wide legs and arms, round cheeks and tummies, large shuffling or rolling movements. Freezing weather: Jack Frost shapes, spiky, dabbing and pointing fingers, jagged elbows, jerky darting and jumping movements.
- Listen to music representing the mood of winter, e.g. Vaughan Williams 'Sinfonia Antarctica'. Make up your own interpretation for heavy, grey skies (soft beaters, taps and rolls on tambour/drum). Icicles sliding off and crashing (glockenspiel or swannee whistle and a cymbal shimmer). Shimmering, frosty leaves (gentle tambourine shakes). Use these ideas to accompany a snowy story or make up a sound picture.
- Look at the group of January songs in *Harlequin* (A & C Black).

Further activities from the book
- Make sets of clothes worn in hot, cold or wet weather. What sorts of materials would be suitable for Peter's snow suit?
- Look at the tracks Peter made in the snow. What other tracks might you see? Try making a bird's foot printer from match sticks or cut pieces of straw. Make a spotter's guide to tracks you could find in the snow - duck, cats, horse, wheels.
- Make a picture sequence showing how Peter may have played in the snow next day. What new, exciting things could he do?
- **Make each arm of the snowflake equal the central number.**

Pirates

ONE-EYED JAKE, Pat Hutchins (Picture Puffin)
I Wish I had a Pirate Suit, Pamela Allen. **The Man whose Mother was a Pirate,** Margaret Mahy.
Who's a Clever Girl then? Rose Impey. **Cowardy, Cowardy Cutlass,** Robin Kingsland.

Collections
A range of cask type containers: lacquered, inlaid, leather and carved boxes, including some with 'jewels'.
Toy boats including those with paddles, rudders, sails, remote control. Pictures of boats from magazines,
books and by famous artists - include some of storms. Newspaper clippings of sea dramas. Pirate costume:
T-shirt, eye patch, wig. Compass, telescope, lenses. Various maps.

Starters
Talk about times when the children may have travelled across water. What size was the craft, how was it
powered and where did they go? Compile a scrap book for the class library of different sorts of craft and
what they are used for: tankers, junks, fishing boats, hovercraft, lifeboat. Collect newspaper cuttings of
sailing/dramatic events (Cowes, Tall Ships race, lifeboat rescues) to add to the scrap book. Brainstorm and
list nautical words. Find out about famous local mariners. Look at the amount of sea on a globe and identify
oceans. Talk about the difference between sea, lake, river. Discuss and plot the journey from school to an
overseas destination. What land/sea would have to be travelled over?

English
- Make up a poem about a pirate on a stormy sea. Each line describes a different aspect, e.g. the wind, sea, consequences for the boat, how the pirate feels, how the storm abates.
- Make a rogues gallery. Include famous pirates you know about, or make up your own, giving apt names and describing infamous deeds.
- Imagine you've just been pulled onto a rescue ship after being marooned for being cheeky to the captain. Tell the story of your time on the island. What did you eat and where did you shelter? Did you try to send any messages? What dangers were there on the island?
- Make a list of six rules to give a pirate crew to keep things running smoothly. How can you make the paper look authentic?
- Send messages using signal flags. Design your own and give a key. Either each flag is a complete message, e.g. 'disease on board keep clear', or use to represent letters of the alphabet or sounds.

Maths
- Draw/make a boat. Give children cards or oral instructions like this: draw a boat with 3 sails, 4 port holes; use Duplo/Lego to make a boat as long as your foot/15cm wide; make a Plasticine boat that balances a toy boat/weighs 100gms.
- Sort boat pictures onto a decision tree, answering yes/no to questions like: has it got a funnel? Has it got sails? Is it engine powered? Is it carrying cargo?
- Make string islands. Take a piece of string (about 50cm to start with) and make into island shapes. What's the biggest/smallest island you can make? How can you check the area? (Fill with objects or place over squared paper.)
- Identikit pirates. How many different pirates can you make using a hat, a beard, an eye patch? e.g. hat only; hat and patch; hat and beard. Increase the combinations by using a scarf, earring, telescope, cutlass, belt.
- **Play a treasure trail game.** Throw dice to show number of squares to move. Pick up treasure as marked on square. How many pieces of gold can you collect in five turns? Change base-board numbers to suit children's ability.

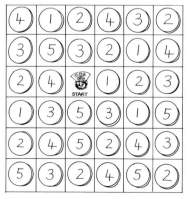

Science

● Explore how different materials float and sink. Incorporate some surprises, e.g. large objects that float, metal objects that float and some that sink. Predict first, then discuss your findings. Make a chart showing: which objects sink quickly; float first then sink; make bubbles as they go down.

● **Make a boat to cross the water tray.** Try out different materials: foil, polystyrene dish, lids, bottles, pieces of wood. Investigate different shaped bases or the number, size and shape of sails. Compare how well they float/move. Find out which will carry the largest cargo (use bricks/cubes). Is there an efficient way of stacking the cargo?

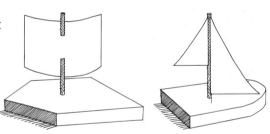

● Investigate materials found on tide lines. Sort into natural (driftwood, pebbles, seaweed) and man-made (bottles, polystyrene, cans). Display the objects/pictures on either side of a tide line. Annotate how they got there and what might happen to them next.

● Use a simple electrical circuit to make a light signal for a pirate's landing cove.

Humanities

● Make a papier mâché island incorporating features like: hills, slope, valley, inlet. Older children can base their island on the contours from a map, building the relief up with cut-out card contour shapes.

● Draw a bird's-eye-view of pirate objects like: wooden cask, hat, toy boat. Display, matching the plan views to the actual objects.

● Play ships and navigators. The 'navigator' uses compass points to 'steer the ship' through the rocky outlets to a safe haven. Use instructions like North 2 paces, South 3.

● Make a 'boats through the ages' timeline. Look at different designs of boats and record your findings on concertina cut-out boat shapes.

● Write a log as a pirate. Include: jobs being done (looking after the armoury, scrubbing decks etc.); food (ships' biscuits, salted meat, rancid butter); health and hygiene (teeth falling out, scurvy); weather conditions; writing home to loved ones; confrontations with other pirate crews; the discovery of a woman pirate on board.

- Draw a cross-section of a pirate ship. Label what each area is used for: goods hold, galley, mess room, officer's cabin, store rooms.

Art and Craft/Design and Technology
- Make pop-up pirates based on famous pirates, or invent your own.

- Make a pirate frieze. Try using water and wash techniques: marbling; wet blotting paper and inks; dry powder paint on wet paper; applying one colour while the other is still wet to get a runny effect. Experiment with different thicknesses of paint and tilting the paper at different angles. Use the results to cut up and form different aspects of the frieze. (See photograph.)
- Make a pirate's treasure chest with a lid that opens, closes and fastens. Investigate the different ways of making hinges.
- Make a collage picture of a treasure island and the surrounding sea. On a separate piece of card, make a pirate boat and find a way of making it move across the sea: slits and tabs, levers.
- Put some 'treasure' at the bottom of the water tray. Devise a way of lifting the sunken treasure without putting your hands in the water.

Music
- Learn 'Pirate King' (*Silly Aunt Sally,* Ward Lock Educational), or a sea shanty from *The Jolly Herring* (A & C Black). As you sing it together make forwards/backwards arm movements - rowing the boat, pulling up the anchor or rigging. Keep a strong, steady rhythm throughout.
- Make the sounds of a storm. Think about sounds the wind, rain and sea might make during a storm: rumble, crash, whoosh, howl. Practise saying these in different ways - short and sharp, soft and mysterious. Try extending the beginning, middle or end of a sound (sssspit, daaarrrk, splashshshsh). Give groups a particular sound and 'conduct' them in a sound storm scape.
- Play short extracts from sea/storm music (Britten's 'Noye's Fludde' or 'Sea Interludes', the Onedin Line theme - Khachaturyan's 'Spartacus'). Can the children spot where the calms and storms are? Invite the children to bring in their own music which feels stormy to them.

Further activities from the book
- Look carefully at the illustrations for the loot One-Eyed Jake had. Make treasure for a decorated chest: jewels, goblets, clothes, jars, gold buttons.
- Make up a simple picture story sequence showing which loads were taken on board and whether or not they sank the pirate ship. In which order were the items/people thrown off as it began to sink?
- Collect some of the objects shown in the book to weigh. Talk about heavier/lighter than, e.g. the banana is heavier than the feather; the goblet is heavier than the spice jar. Older children could use standard units to record, e.g., the necklace is 10gm heavier than the small bell.
- Make up a delicious recipe the cook might serve to put One-Eyed Jake in a good mood. This could be based on some of the fruits shown. Alternatively, make up a truly awful dish to pay him back for being so nasty.
- What might some of the characters in the book dream of doing in happier times? Consider the people on the passenger ships, the fishermen, the cat. Put the ideas into dream bubbles.

Patterns

THE PATCHWORK QUILT, Valerie Flournoy (Picture Puffin)
The Patchwork Cat, Nicola Bayley/William Mayne. **The Quilt,** Ann Jonas. **Elmer,** David McKee.

Collections
Make a display table of patchwork and tessellation: bedspread, tea cosies, clothing, wrapping papers, board games (e.g. chess, draughts) and posters, magazines, catalogue pictures showing tessellating patterns in the environment - bricks, roof and floor tiles, piece of honeycomb.

Starters
Help the children to understand that patterns are regular, repeated shapes. Find patterns around the school - windows, bricks, floor and roof tiles, large apparatus. Look at decorative patterns on children's clothes, and objects from the display collection (e.g. fabrics, pottery). Discuss patterning on wrapping papers: how many items are in the pattern? In which order are they repeated? Focus on directional language: across, sideways, diagonal - are there any stripes, spirals or spots? Think about life patterns: birthdays; order of events; life-cycles in nature.

English

- Make an alphabet frieze for a nursery wall. Try giving it a theme - animals, toys, food.
- Make a class/individual diary as a way of recording the pattern of the children's day/week. Talk about the kinds of things people put in their diaries - events, reminders, feelings, secrets.
- Rhymes around a circle. Start with a word (hill) and take turns to find a rhyme (frill, mill, pill). Use these ideas to make an illustrated book of rhymes, e.g. 'The fat cat', 'frog on a log'.
- Make a peep-hole pattern book. Draw some pictures with a strong pattern theme. Look through the cut-out shape for clues, e.g. is the spiky pattern a rooftop or a crocodile's back?
- **Decorate palindromes with handwriting patterns and make a hanging display.**

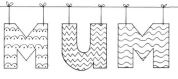

- How many words can be made from the word PATTERN? Help by grouping words with the same letter strings (at, sat, pat, rat). Make a score points system for words with 2,3,4 letters.
- Compose some alliterative descriptions of classmates or other people the children know well, e.g. 'lovely, laughing Leon', 'beautiful Betty', 'kind Kate'. Compile ideas into a book of 'Friendly Folk'.
- **Create some calligrams.**

Maths
- Make sequences for others to continue (or find the missing piece). Use: buttons, crayons, junk solids, logi-blocks etc. Set a challenge to older children - how many different properties can you use to sequence straws (length, colour, thickness, orientation, plastic/paper)?
- Build a tower with 6 interlocking cubes. Record how many different ways you can split it into 2 parts. Continue the pattern by looking at other number towers.
- **Find all the dominoes with spots totalling 4.** How many are there in the '4 spot' set? Draw or make a table, showing how many dominoes are in the 1, 2, 3....12 spot sets.

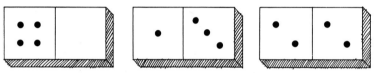

- Make instructions for movement patterns: use directional words like: right, left, whole, half turn. Draw the pattern, then try it out on a friend. Adapt to use with robotic toys/screen logo.
- Create patterns of shapes which tessellate. Can the children make a tessellation using two (or more) different shapes - triangle and square; oblong and square?
- Make a set of pentominoes (joining the edges of five squares). Can the children fit them all together as a quilt?
- **Make square number patterns with interlocking cubes, dotty or squared paper. Try triangular patterns in the same way.**

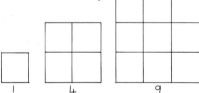
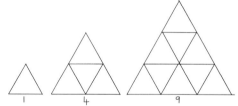

Science/Design and Technology
- Make a feely box to develop the children's language and awareness of pattern and texture: rough, smooth, spiky, furry. Can they find pairs of fabric pieces by touch alone?
- Chart the pattern of growth of a runner bean.
- Make a 6-10 piece jigsaw for someone younger than you. Design an envelope to keep the pieces safe.
- Talk about how Braille patterns help those with poor eyesight. Punch/prick holes into a range of materials (tissue, cartridge paper, card, tin foil, cling film, plastic). Investigate which are easiest to 'read'. Do any of the holes close up with use?
- Stitch a rag book for a toddler. Choose interesting patterns, prints and textures.
- Make a simple model (about six pieces) of, e.g. junk box robot, Duplo tower, card glider. Put together a kit for a friend so they can make one just the same. Include the pieces needed and an assembly pattern (picture sequence, labels, diagram of outline shapes and arrows).

Humanities
- Use pictures and photographs to make a family portrait gallery. Can the children place them in generation order? Make some labels and/or a gallery guide (age, where they live, favourite pastimes).
- Go for a walk or look at and discuss pictures of environmental patterns. Where can you find regular or repeating patterns (tiles, arches, paving stones etc)? Take rubbings, sketches or photographs to make a picture map of 'local patterns' sites.

- Make a school quilt, or wall-hanging, to commemorate an important school occasion (see photograph).
- Look closely at and discuss 'patterning' on pictures, photographs and artefacts, e.g. African pottery, Roman mosaics, illuminated manuscripts, story friezes. Discuss the similarities and differences. Can a partner match your descriptions to the objects?
- Use photographs, pictures and maps to discuss patterns in geographical features. Look for evidence of natural/man-made patterns, e.g. straight roads, canals, town layout and landscape features, rivers and coastlines. Can the children notice cluster patterns - village/city; forest/copse?

Art and Craft
- **Make concertina cut-out borders.**

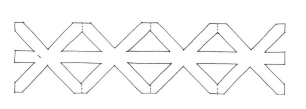  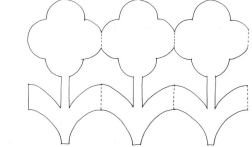

- Thread or stick a sequence of junk/natural materials on to lengths of ribbon or wool. Try buttons, seeds, feathers, lace scraps etc. Hang the patterns in groups, fastened on to a covered hoop.
- **Design your own tessellation template.** Make a pattern by repeatedly drawing round the shape, or cut out paper/fabric shapes to fit together.

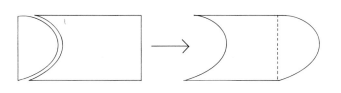 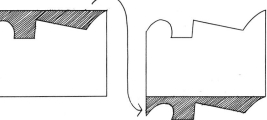

- Show and discuss pictures, photographs and objects with mosaic patterns. Make individual tiles from sticky paper/magazine squares. Use a tessellating shape for each tile's backing paper and piece together as a wall mosaic or frieze.

Music
- Play extracts of music with contrasting tempo (rap, brass band march, lullaby). Can the children clap in time? Accent the strong beat: CLAP, tap, tap, tap.
- Draw a pattern of long and short sounds (like Morse code). Can a partner play it? Find a way of showing when to play loudly or softly.
- Sit in a circle and chant a voice pattern, e.g. CH, ber, ber, ber - stress the CH sound to help the children feel a regular pulse. After practice, pass the pattern around the circle: take turns to say one sound of the sequence, keeping the accent on CH.

Further activities from the book
- Make a touch picture for Grandma to feel, rather than look at. Focus the children's attention on materials which give a raised surface - wood shavings, crushed shells, bottle tops.
- Design a patchwork quilt 'kit box'. Allow space/dividers for everything you need: needles, cotton, fabric, scissors.
- 'A quilt won't forget', so Grandma says. How else can we remember things - photographs, sharing reminiscences, mementoes, diaries? Compile a class/individual collection of memories to record: today, this week, a special event.
- Test whether some fabrics wear out more quickly than others. How many sandpaper rubs does it take to make a hole in the material?

Materials and Waste

STIG OF THE DUMP, Clive King (Puffin)
The Iron Man, Ted Hughes. *Charlie's House,* Reviva Schermbrucker.
Professor Noah's Spaceship, Brian Wildsmith. *Dinosaurs and all that Rubbish,* Michael Foreman.

Collections

Stone: include some crystal/gem stones, pottery, china. Metal: ring pulls, nuts, springs, foil, coins, piping. Glass: bottles and jars, marbles, thermometer, vase. Plastic: include rigid and flexible types. Wood and paper: showing grains, knots and bark, newspapers, cards, bags. Fibres: natural - wool, cotton, silk; man-made - nylon, Courtelle, Terylene. Pictures of scrap yards and recycling banks.

Starters

Beginning with what the children are wearing, and familiar classroom objects, sort your materials collection by: colour, texture, use, natural/man-made. Play 'spot the odd one out' games. Use a 'feely' tray (include some sand, polished stone, bark, damp clay etc.) to encourage children to describe what objects feel like. Focus on opposites, e.g. smooth/rough, warm/cold. Now look closely - are the objects patterned or plain, shiny or dull? Which ones make a ringing sound when tapped? Talk about the suitability of materials for certain jobs (see English). Look at what's been discarded in the class bin today and discuss the sorts of things people throw away, and why. Handle only clean rubbish and provide children with plastic gloves. What do the children know about recycling?

English

● Take two items from your collection (use more later) and play a game of 'Link it'. Can the children describe how they are the same, e.g. both feel cold, smooth, bend, are made of plastic. Try identifying what's different about them.

● Draw an alien from the land of Wastenot. Describe all the waste materials it's made from - shiny bottle top eyes, arms of burnt toast crusts, etc.

● Talk about what a litter bug is. Act out the scene of the litter bug caught 'red handed' by the rubbish detective. Make comic strips showing what happened.

● Make a 'What would happen if...' book, based on your talk about why materials are suited to particular jobs. What if flannels were made of tin foil; roads of play dough; lamp shades of chocolate? Display in two frames - the 'what if' picture next to the described consequences.

● Imagine if rubbish bins were never emptied, or you kept all your old toys and clothes. **Make a build-up sequence book with captions,** describing what might happen over time. The final page shows the rubbish stockpile.

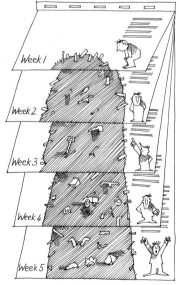

Maths

● Match lids to various sized bottles and jars. Can the children do this by touch?
● Unpack junk boxes to find their nets. Make a similar net from Polydron or paper, and display by matching these to the complete box.

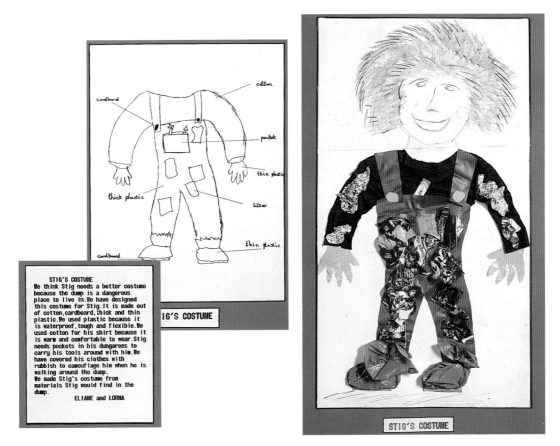

STIG'S COSTUME
We think Stig needs a better costume because the dump is a dangerous place to live in. We have designed this costume for Stig. It is made out of cotton, cardboard, thick and thin plastic. We used plastic because it is waterproof, tough and flexible. We used cotton for his shirt because it is warm and comfortable to wear. Stig needs pockets in his dungarees to carry his tools around with him. We have covered his clothes with rubbish to camouflage him when he is walking around the dump.
We made Stig's costume from materials Stig would find in the dump.

ELIANE and LORNA

- Estimate, then find the amount of paper needed to wrap a box efficiently without waste. How accurate were the estimates? Do the same for a range of box sizes. Display the box next to the paper used to cover it.
- How many different 'crate' arrangements can the children make with twelve bottles? How many columns will there be if they have 2, 3, 4 rows?
- Survey how much paper is thrown away in class (or the newspapers, magazines and comics taken by a family) in a week. How will the waste be measured, e.g. by number/size of sheets, or weight? How much is there at the end of the week?

Science

- Observe the differences between wet and dry objects: sponge, feather, seaweed, clay, chalk. Give the children two examples of each of the materials to be observed. Leave one dry, and put the other in water. Record before and after observations describing colour, texture, strength, shape.
- Bury some rubbish to examine later. Use marker sticks for various items, e.g. nail, can, tissue, twig, crisp bag. Leave for 2-4 weeks. Talk about how the rubbish has changed and display as a set of 'look what happened to our rubbish' pictures and captions.
- How can you make rubbish smaller? (Use clean junk, which can be crushed, folded, flattened, stacked or placed inside each other.)
- **Investigate the properties of materials.** Provide a range of materials (polythene bag, envelope, tin foil, clay, wood, Plasticine, glass jar, cotton fabric, metal can) and test for properties such as: hard, smooth, does it twist...? Record like this:

	soft	hard	rough	smooth	shiny	dull	bend	twist	squash	stretch	see through it
wood	x	✓	✓	x	x	✓	x	x	x	x	x
clay	✓	x	x	✓	✓						

- Test the effect of heat on different materials. Put candles, toffee, straws, wax crayon, plastic, wooden or metal spoons, one at a time, into a jug of hot water. Do they soften, feel warm to the touch? Make pairs of labelled pictures to display the results.

Humanities

- Go for a litter spot in and around the school. Predict the sorts of rubbish you'll see and which areas are likely to be heavily littered. Are bins in the right place? Does the school need more, and how can people be encouraged to use them?
- Make a local guide showing how to find the bottle/can banks, paper collection points etc. You could include a small map, a photograph or picture of the collection point and how it is used.
- Use pictures and artefacts to look at what we used before plastic. Display and label plastic buttons, handles, recorders etc. next to their older versions.
- Make a flow diagram showing a simple sequence of what happens in recycling processes, e.g. from the bottle bank to cullet to new green glass bottles. Do the same for paper, compost or cans.
- Create the contents of rubbish bins for a variety of characters, e.g. young couple with a new baby and a puppy; make-up demonstrator who grows all her own vegetables and loves chocolate; dressmaker who works at home and reads lots of newspapers and magazines.

Art and Craft/Design and Technology
- Weaving waste: **take an interesting shaped twig and weave waste materials in and around it.**

- Brainstorm ideas for using old magazines. Try making games cards (Lotto, Snap, Happy Families); a picture scrap book for a sick toddler; badges; framed pictures. Show the ideas on a 'How we reused our magazines' display.
- Try making sculptures of all one material, e.g. a plastics sculpture using: bags and nets to scrunch, tear, cut and stretch. Try making a magnetic sculpture, using a large bar magnet and paper clips, nails, pins, small magnets.
- Design a waste bin for the classroom, bedroom or kitchen. Think about what materials to use, measurements and stability. Can it be emptied easily? Does it need to keep in smells?
- Make a window decoration, e.g. a mobile, stick-on or painted picture. Think about which materials let light through (Cellophane, tissue, greaseproof paper).

Music

- Take one type of material and find out what kinds of sounds you can make from it. Begin with a sheet of newspaper for each child. After exploration, ask volunteers to explain how they made a sound - blow, rustle, snap, tear, rip, scrunch etc. The rest of the class echoes this movement and sound. Inject a challenge - can the children take turns around the circle to make a sound no one has made before? What sounds can you make with a card tube or plastic sweet trays?
- *The Green Umbrella* (A & C Black) is a book of stories, songs and poems, all with environmental themes. Other songs with conservation themes: 'Pollution Calypso', 'Keep the Countryside Tidy' (*Every Colour Under the Sun,* Ward Lock Educational).
- 'The Tidy Song' (*Tinderbox,* A & C Black) - make up verses about keeping a classroom, street or garden tidy.

Further activities from the book

- Use natural materials (feathers, twigs, stones) to make Stig cave paintings. Depict Barney's descent into the pit, or another memorable event.
- Make your play area into Stig's dump. Provide a 'useful box' containing pieces of tubing, a broken sieve, bent wheels etc. for the children to design and make their own Stig inventions.
- Sing 'Stig of the Dump' (*Sing A Story,* A & C Black) - a song based on the novel.
- Using only clean waste materials, design and make a garment for Stig to wear on rainy days. Children should design the garment first, and list the sorts of waste materials they will need. Which of these materials has the best water-repellent properties? (See photograph.)
- Make a countdown calendar to show how many days children would have to wait to visit Grandma during half-term, Christmas or Summer holidays.
- Compare Stig the stone age boy, with 'present day' Barney. Put the two characters in the centre of a picture and annotate with labels showing differences in homes, food, clothes, tools.

Knights and Castles

Make and play Sir Tumbleweed's musical dragon

TUMBLEWEED, Dick King-Smith (Puffin)
Meg's Castle, Helen Nicoll. *King Nonn the Wiser,* Colin McNaughton.
The Knight who was Afraid of the Dark, B.Shook Hazen.
Sir Gawain and the Green Knight, retold by Selina Hastings.

Collections

Pictures and post cards of castles around the world, knights and dragons, period costume, Bayeux Tapestry. A busy 'inside the castle' picture, a model fort.

Starters

Use the collection materials, and what the children already know, to talk about what a castle is (a big building with especially strong defences). Compare pictures of ruined castles with those still inhabited today. Discuss who lived in castles then (kings, noblemen and their servants) and now. Identify features - portcullis, turrets, moat, drawbridge, keep - and relate to common words like cellar, front door, tower. Consider what it may have been like to live in a castle (see English). Try to visit a local castle/museum.

English

● Look closely at a busy castle picture and talk about what's going on in and around the building: horse and carts for transport, a feast, drawing water from a well, entertainers. Act out what some of the people might be doing and saying to each other, e.g. helping a knight into his armour; a serving boy at the feast.
● Retell a knight's story using puppets or some simple props.
● Invent some names for knights. Can the children make them reflect brave deeds and/or the knight's characteristics (Fergus the Forgetful, Rufus the Red). Older children could use alliteration.
● Make some word chain mail. Take a three letter word, change one letter to make a new one.

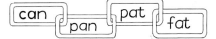

● Adapt for words with four letters, or give the first or last word in the chain.
● Make a jester's joke book. Older children could give it a historical flavour, e.g. change elephant jokes to dragon jokes.

● Think of a dreamy wish for a knight or other character from your book. Display as a 'Castles in the Air' frieze, showing characters and their castle-shaped dream bubbles.

Maths

● Use sand castles and flags for: matching 1:1; grouping and regrouping (e.g. 9 flags = 1+8; 7+2); sharing flags between 2/3/4 castles; odd and even numbers
● Make a castle with cones and cylinders, using either solid or paper shapes. How can you make taller/shorter, wider/narrower paper cylinders?
● Number chains - complete the pattern, fill in the missing numbers.

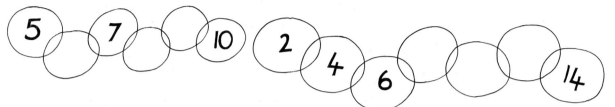

● In pairs, take 8 quarter circles: 4 red, 4 green.
Make circular shields with them. Can you make exactly the same pattern shield as your partner? How many different designs can you make?

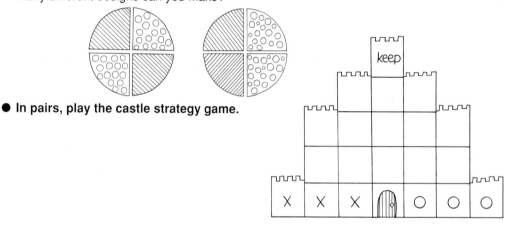

● **In pairs, play the castle strategy game.**

Place your knights in starting positions as shown. Take turns to move any of the pieces, forwards or sideways one square. The aim is to get all your knights into the keep, blocking your opponent if possible. Adapt rules by: restricting the direction or number of places knights are allowed to move; introducing jumping over and capturing pieces.
● Cut out some square shield shapes from squared paper. Using only one colour, shade in half the shield. Take another shield and colour half in a different way. How many different shields can you make?
● Use squared or dotty paper to make spiral staircase numbers. Explore a 1,4,2 staircase. Start at any point and move 1 square forwards, make a quarter turn (clockwise). Move forward 4 squares, turn, 2 squares forward, turn... keep repeating the 1,4,2 sequence. Can you make spirals with other number groups? Try doing this using logo graphics.

Science/Design and Technology

● Get the children to look carefully at a picture of a castle and model the features in sand, construction toys or junk materials. Focus on the number of towers, shape of battlements, size of arrow slits.
● Find out which materials are best for draughty castle windows. Make a simple card 'window frame'. Place the frame between a lit candle in a bowl of sand, and an air pump (bicycle/balloon). Take care near naked flames. Test the uncovered frame and then try out different coverings - net, paper, wool etc. Does the flame ever go out completely?
● Investigate how to stop chain mail going rusty. What can the children suggest to cover a nail (PVA glue, varnish, Sellotape, butter, wax)? Put untreated and treated nails in jars of water and chart the results. Which anti-rust materials might have been used by the knights themselves?
● Design and make a drawbridge that moves up and down. Encourage the children to think carefully about how to make moving parts. Can they make one strong enough to squash a Plasticine dragon?

● Make a castle shape out of a piece of card. Can the children devise a way of making a knight pop up and down over the battlements; or an arrow shoot from a slit?

Humanities
● Look at all the rooms/areas inside a castle. Where would you find the dungeons, kitchen, Great Hall? Make a cross section, with pictures and labels, showing the kinds of activities that happened in the various rooms.
● Make a 'Then and Now' book comparing life in a castle with present day facilities and comforts. Use pairs of pictures to show the differences between: heating (open fires - central heating); lighting (candles - light bulb); entertainments, clothes, hygiene.
● Talk about how heraldic symbols say something important about a person or family. Children can make shields showing something special about themselves or their family. Older children could research the origins of their own names.
● Design the ideal geographical site for a castle. Show if it is on high ground, near a steep cliff, near a water supply.

Art and Craft
● Make a castle of rubbings. Take rubbings of different textures (bricks, grilles, wallpaper etc). Cut out castle features and arrange.
● Spatter chain mail: arrange different sized 'washers' (metal or card) on paper in a pleasing chain mail design. Spatter-print over them (use paint-filled brush and card scraper). Remove, rearrange and spatter again (use silvers, greys and whites).
● Take castle/knights monoprints. Try printing on different kinds of paper: coloured Cellophane, crêpe, tissue (as a stain-glass window).
● Look at a picture of the Bayeux tapestry. Make up your own picture story in a similar style for an adventure based on a knight's book.

Music
● Make the sound effects of a spooky castle: creaking doors, rattling chains, scratching mice. Explore the different ways you can make raps, taps, knocks and bangs. Try a background of vocal sounds: whistles, moans, screeches. Add pauses for maximum effect.
● Sing some songs from *Phantasmagoria* (A & C Black): 'Excalibur', 'Songs of Dragons and Knights', 'Three Ghosts'. Others in this collection can easily be adapted to fit a knights/dragons theme.
● Listen to early traditional dance music played on original instruments (shawm, crumhorn, hurdy-gurdy). Try making up some simple dances to these, e.g. 3 steps to the right, knees bend, repeat to the left; 4 steps in to the middle, 4 out again. Make this into a castle entertainment for a feast by adding jugglers and acrobats.

Further activites from the book
● List five characteristics of Sir Tumbleweed, and five opposite traits alongside side them, showing the qualities of the traditional knight.
● Make two marbled/textured dragons, one red, one green (representing the kind and the nasty). Put appropriate describing words on each of the dragons.
● Design a poster to promote a jousting competition.
● Make a board game that illustrates the sequence of events in the book, e.g. Tumbleweed meets the witch (move on two places); Taffy helps out (have another go). The winner is the first person to get to the wedding party.
● Make up and then act out an alternative ending to the book.
● Talk about how the witch, lion and unicorn helped the nervous Sir Tumbleweed. What ideas can the children think up to help a clumsy dragon? Write the ideas on 'scales' to build up a picture of the clumsy dragon.

Headgear

THE QUANGLE WANGLE'S HAT, Edward Lear (Heinemann)
Ho for a Hat!, William Jay Smith. **Jennie's Hat,** Ezra Jack Keats.
The Extraordinary Hatmaker, Malcolm Carrick.

Collections
Job-related headgear: fireman, astronaut, nurse, welder etc. Other headgear: wizard's hat, wigs, crown, night cap, jester's hat, masks. Soft toys associated with hats (Paddington bear, cartoon characters). Three or four basic shapes for designer hats (See English/Role Play), e.g. pill box, safari, sun hat. Removable trimmings, e.g. braids, bells, ribbons, cotton reels, badges and logos, feathers, cones.

Starters
Look at and discuss any hats the children wear to school. Why do people wear them (protection from the elements, part of cultural tradition, identification, safety)? Do the children wear hats at any other time during the week - perhaps for Brownies, Cubs, swimming, cycling? Show the range on a collage or in a class catalogue. Talk about the hats seen on the way to school (police, traffic warden, lollipop people, bus drivers, in shop windows). Add appropriate hat pictures to a simple map of the route from home to school. Draw on the cultural diversity of your class to talk about hats worn for special occasions: weddings, festivals, carnivals. Discuss hats worn by characters in fiction and on television. Brainstorm and list other types of headgear: masks, goggles, veils, headphones etc.

English/Role Play
● Let the children put on special occasion or job related hats and mime whom they have become, what they are doing or where they are going. Can their friends guess?
● **Have a hat design studio** (see Collections) and use in imaginative play. Invent an appropriate studio name. Make your own designer labels, carrier bags and receipt pads. Children order, either verbally or on request slips, a hat for a special occasion, e.g. a theme party (water, animal, fantasy). Designers use the removable trimmings to create their customers' special hats.

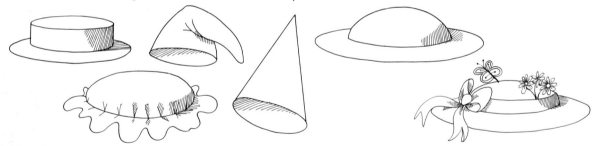

● List as many uses as you can for an old hat: nest, basket, flower pot etc., and illustrate what it would look like. Who/what might use it?
● Write invitations for a carnival or fancy dress party. Decorate with a border of hats to give the guests an idea of what they might wear.
● Compile a glossary of hats (beret, bowler, top). You could use this hat word bank to make word searches and crosswords.
● Think of some well-known phrases or sayings associated with hats: a feather in your cap; I'll eat my hat; to talk through one's hat etc. Make a simple story sequence to illustrate one of them.

Maths
● Match hats to different sized toys and dolls. Talk about too big, too small, tight, fits, covers.
● Sort out the shelves in a hat shop. Each shelf represents a different type of headgear: uniform, sport, protection, celebrations. Use ideas from magazines, catalogues, comics, photographs and drawings.
● Make hats based on solid shapes - cones (wizard, coolie); cylinders (chef, fez, top hat). Talk about the properties of solid and plane shapes, segments, how to take careful measurements, make wider, shorter, narrower or taller.
● Use your hat collection to place hats in order of size - length, width, height, circumference, weight.

THE ORIENT CALF'S HAT

We have designed and made a hat for
the Orient Calf. We looked
carefully at the patterns and
colours on the clothes of the Calf
and made a hat to match. We think
the Calf's favourite colour is pink,
so we used a lot of pink in the hat.
We think the Orient Calf would enjoy
wearing this hat.

● Make a chart of the children's head sizes (circumference). If possible, compare baby and adult sizes - are the differences large or small? What other head measurements can you take?

Science

● Identify hats by touch only (eyes shut) and describe: size, shape, rough, smooth, hairy, tickly, scratchy, hard etc.

● **Predict, then test, how well different fabrics keep out the rain.** How can you be sure they all get the same amount of water (fair test)?

● How can fabrics be made more water resistant? Try PVA glue, wax, nail varnish. Investigate how long fabrics take to dry.

● **Use your collection of headgear to look at care labels and washing instructions.** Test some of the materials. Display like this:

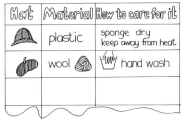

Hat	Material	How to care for it
🎩	plastic	sponge dry keep away from heat
🧶	wool 🧶	🪣 hand wash

Humanities

● Using photographs if possible, research hats worn by members of the children's own families: for weddings, BMX helmets, Brownies/Cubs, etc. Invite older members of the family in to share their memories of special hat-wearing occasions. Make a book and a tape and match the reminiscences to the people/photographs.

● Choose three pictures showing hot, cold, rainy weather. Match appropriate headgear to the pictures. Give reasons for choice, e.g. it's made from cotton which is best for keeping cool; it's furry so it keeps you warm; it's made from plastic to keep out the rain.

● Use pictures of hats from travel agents' brochures and postcards etc, showing hats around the world. Cut out the faces wearing hats and add speech bubbles such as: 'My name is Lee Min. I come from China. I'm wearing a dragon's mask.' Give reasons why particular headgear is worn (climate, celebrations, traditional costume etc). Put all the faces together to make a wall display.

Art and Craft/Design and Technology

● Select a hat from your display collection. Choose an appropriate sized container for it from the junk box and add handles and a lid; or, design and make a solid shape box to protect a hat from damage. Can the children make the box so it will stack?

● Make a head scarf for a friend or soft toy. Use a cotton square and decorate it with fabric crayons, printed pattern, tie-dye or batik.

● **Make a hat to fit a friend from a sheet of newspaper.** The children could go on to give oral or written step-by-step instructions so others can make one just like it.

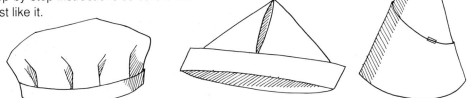

● Make some hat trimmings. Limit materials to, say, 3 lengths of ribbon, 2 pipe cleaners, a piece of lace, feathers and a cork.

● Cut some hat pictures in two along a line of symmetry and stick one half on a piece of plain paper. Children draw the other half, paying special attention to shape, colour and technique used in the original picture.

● Design and make a Heath Robinson type piece of headgear which does something amazing: wipes spectacles; holds a packed lunch or train tickets in a secret compartment; has dials to aid an underwater explorer.

Music

● Learn 'My Hat it Has Three Corners' (*Okki-Tokki-Unga*, A & C Black). Sing it with actions replacing the words 'hat', 'three', 'corners'. Try replacing these mimed words with instruments: tambourine for 'hat,' triangle for 'three', wood blocks for 'corners'.

● Children sit in a circle, each with an instrument in front of them. A hat is passed round the circle from head to head as the children sing (to the tune of 'London Bridge') 'Take the hat and pass it on —- how shall we play?' Whoever is wearing the hat as the song ends, decides how everyone plays their instrument: loud and slowly, quickly and quietly.

Further activities from the book

● Invent fantastical collage creatures of your own. Make up alliterative or rhyming names.

● Choose an instrument and then make up a noise for a specific creature, e.g. what noises might the Olympian Bear make when walking, dreaming, laughing, excited?

● Can the children draw pictures of what they think Quangle Wangle might have looked like? Older children could put their ideas into a Wanted or Missing Person poster.

● Plan, design and make a suitable hat (to fit child or a soft toy), for a favourite Quangle Wangle character. Look carefully at the creature and make the hat complement both its patterning and physical characteristics, e.g. how do you make allowances for the Orient Calf's horns and what kind of decoration would it like? (See photograph.)

● Characterise some of the Quangle Wangle creatures and make up conversations between them, e.g. Is the Fimble Fowl clumsy, moody, noisy? Is the Golden Grouse proud, timid?

● The hat was 102 feet wide. What would this look like in metres? How does this measurement compare with the size of the playing field/playground/hall? How many children could fit under a hat that size?

Seaside

SPOT GOES ON HOLIDAY, Eric Hill (Heinemann)
The Bears who went to the Seaside, Susanna Gretz. **Lucy and Tom at the Seaside,** Shirley Hughes.
Come Away from the Water Shirley, John Burningham. **The Sea Egg,** Lucy M. Boston.

Collections

Travel agents' brochures, tourist information for coastal resorts, postcards. Items taken on seaside holidays past and present: suitcase and contents, beach mat, towels, arm bands, buckets and spades, sunglasses. Souvenirs and mementoes of seaside holidays in Britain and abroad. Shells, seaweed, rocks, driftwood.

Starters

Who has been to the seaside and in which country was it? Can the children find these on a map/globe/atlas? Share stories about day trips and longer seaside holidays. List the sort of accommodation they stayed in: caravan, camp site, bed and breakfast. Find out about different forms of water: ocean, lake, river, waterfall. Look at a globe and talk about the area covered by sea. Establish that it is salt water containing sea creatures, and has tides. Research marine life: fish, shell fish, jelly fish, plants, coral. Cut out pictures and label as for exhibits in a marine centre. Consider geographical features: terrain (cliffs and seabed), caves, the difference between town, country, and coast.

English/Role Play

● What might people be saying to each other as they play in the sea? 'Look at me'; 'I'm shivering'; 'Stop splashing'. Put the exclamations into speech bubbles and display as a frieze, or take the lines and put them together as an 'It's fun in the sea' poem.

● Turn your play area, or play house, into a travel agency. Role play agent and clients wanting to plan and book a seaside holiday. What's needed to make the agency look authentic and welcoming? Seating areas and a work station for the counter clerk, signs in different languages, posters, booking forms, telephone, timetables and directories. Think up a good name for your company.

● Write a 'Whatever next!' postcard listing seaside surprises, e.g. seagull pinched my sandwiches; the octopus pulled me into the rock pool; the crab nipped my toe.

- Make up a story about an underwater expedition: imagine going down into the murky depths, a shadow appears at the opening of a cavern ... What could it be? Display the stories in a zig-zag book in the shape of a diving vessel.
- Make up a short Punch and Judy script and use simple puppets or a taped recording to act out the scene.

Maths
- Shell sort: match the shells found in fiction/non fiction books and pictures to the real thing. How many different ways can you sort shells: curved, ridged, smooth, flat, colour, size, pattern.
- Sequence with shells: continue a pattern, spot the odd one out, fill in the gap.
- Compare the capacity of buckets in different ways: pour sand from one to another; weigh sand-filled buckets; fill different sized buckets with a common unit, e.g. cups or yoghurt pots.
- Compare different sized/shaped sand timers. What can you do in the time it takes for the sand to run through? e.g. build —- sand castles; count/thread —- shells; write your name in the sand —- times.
- Counting and number patterns using seaside objects: 1 crab has 2 claws, 2 crabs have 4 claws; 1 star fish has 5 arms, 2 star fish have 10, etc.
- Make graphs showing the different types of seaside accommodation the children have stayed in, or the transport taken to holiday resorts.
- Use a catalogue to buy a child's seaside holiday kit spending no more than £50.

Science
- Use sieves to separate objects from dry sand. Try different sized sieves (tea strainer, colander, toaster grill). Which ones work best for large/small shells and pebbles? Relate findings to shrimp and fishing nets.

- Find out about seaside animals and plants. Think about what belongs to sea, land and sky. **Show your findings in a lift-the-flap book.** Each page may show a different aspect of the seaside, e.g. cliffs - lift the flap to reveal nesting birds. Do the same for the shore line, in the sea, rock pool, breakers. Older children could give extra data under the flaps.

- Alongside actual weather charts, keep a record of seaweed predictions: moist and flexible = approaching rain; hard and dry = fair weather. Compare the forecast and the actual weather.
- Seaside foods: what are they (shell fish, fish, samphire)? Where are they found (sea, breakers, fish farms, countries)? Make scallop-shaped recipe cards to show how such foods are used.

Humanities
- **Sort pictures into seaside resorts and other resorts.** Older children could include some that are less obvious (no visible beach) and find out if they are inland or coastal. Which are local, in Britain or abroad? Display as a post card rack.

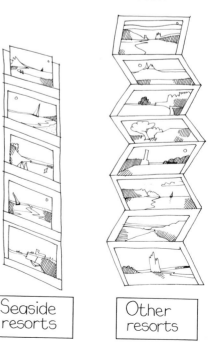

- Where is the nearest seaside resort to you? Display as a tourist information board showing a map, how to get there, and information about main attractions.

Seaside resorts

Other resorts

- Make a post card timeline. Order seaside post cards/photographs/pictures into a timeline by looking for historical clues: type of picture and colours; are the clothes like ours? How busy are the streets? Type of transport. Older children could look more carefully at features like: bands in pleasure gardens, Punch and Judy shows, bathing machines. Discuss the continuity of past and present.
- Make a model showing what a Victorian pier might have been used for. How might boats have used it? What entertainment was on offer (café, fortune teller, camera obscura)?

Art and Craft/Design and Technology
- Make a large wall frieze of an underwater scene. Use standard sized sheets for the children to create their individual water scenes. Use real sand, sandpaper, shingle, pebbles, shells, textured paper for seaweed fronds, anemones and tiny crustaceans. Place side by side to make a large picture. The finished work could be used as a backdrop for mobiles of sea creatures to hang in front of the scene.
- Make a seaside souvenir: paint and decorate pebble creatures; shell covered boxes; play dough/clay gifts; jewellery and wall plates.
- Design a sunbathing towel for a soft toy. Think about fabric, size, and the sort of decoration it might like. Try adding handles so it can be folded or rolled and carried. Are any other fasteners necessary?
- Look closely at sand under magnifiers. Mix sand-coloured paint to make pointillist seaside pictures.
- Make a pair of sunglasses for yourself or a doll. How can they be made to stay on the ears? Make a display stand for the glasses.

Music
- Use seaside objects as sound makers. Fill lidded tubs with sand, pebbles, or small shells. Use as shakers, or roll/tip them from end to end. String shells/dry seaweed together to make rattles or make a shell mobile. Scrape a beater along a large scallop shell, or gently tap two together (like coconut shells). Explore the range of sounds you can make with these. Look at a seaside picture, and talk about the sounds it suggests. Use the instruments to make: water lapping, roaring waves and surf, gulls and moving shingle.
- Sit children in a circle. You repeat the word 'shell' showing the children how to keep a steady pulse. Point to each child in turn around the circle, until all the children are chanting 'shell'. Why did the sound swell? Can you make it swell and drop again?
- Sing: 'Packing up song', 'Just in Case', 'Silly Aunt Sally' (*Silly Aunt Sally*, Ward Lock Educational); 'Take Me to the Seaside', 'Holiday in Spain' (*Harlequin*, A & C Black).

Further Activities from the book
- Look carefully at the beach shop that Spot visited. Set up one like it using your display materials and any items you've made. Alternatively, have a souvenir shop or ice cream van.
- Fit a range of objects into a beach bag. What's the best way to make them all fit? Can the towel be rolled or folded? Will any objects fit inside each other? Try using larger/smaller bags.
- Look at Spot's rubber ring. Talk about other inflatable objects used at the seaside: beach balls, lilos, marker buoys, life belts. Consider water safety. What should we remember when near the water? Draw, print or paint rubber rings and on each of them write one key safety point.

- **Create a Spot story board.** Either individually or in groups, children draw/paint a busy picture incorporating: breakers, sand castles, sea, people, animals, toys. Draw and cut out Spot and put on a card strip. Cut out slots in the seaside scene so that he can be made to pop up in front of the shop, behind the breakwater, under the beach mat. Use to talk about 'Where is Spot hiding?' or make up more elaborate stories.

Houses and Homes

MISS BRICK THE BUILDER'S BABY, A. Ahlberg/C. McNaughton (Puffin)
The Village of Round and Square Houses, Ann Grifalconi. **Our House,** Emma & Paul Rogers.
The Three Pigs, Tony Ross. **The Twig Thing,** Jan Mark.

Collections

Details of houses from estate agents. Labelled photographs and drawings of a range of houses: flat, terrace, tent, houseboat. Include some of the children's own homes. Pictures and postcards of other homes children may have stayed in on holiday, and those which give a historical insight into your locality. Bricks showing a range of colours, sizes, decoration and function. Carpet pieces, lino tiles, wallpaper books, fabric samples for furnishings. DIY tools or those associated with plumbers, carpenters, electricians etc.

Starters

Talk about what a house/home is. Use the pictures in your collection to talk about similarities and differences in house styles, materials, age, size, gardens. Make 'before and after' diagrams showing changes made to rooms in the children's own homes - new furniture, extensions, conservatories etc. Discuss and record services needed in different rooms: water, heating, lighting. What would it be like without these things? Make up slogans/posters about safety in the home. Go out on local walks looking at doors and windows for history clues. Look at road names, numbering systems, building materials. Invite people who work in the building trade to talk to the children about their jobs.

English/Role Play

● **Discuss what is special about children's own houses.** Recap on generalities like 'all houses have doors, windows, walls'. Remind the children that some houses have a chimney, garden, stairs. Pinpoint what's special about 'my house': a squeaky door, a special place to rest when not well, a fish pond etc. You could display like this:

● Use blankets or old drapes to create a tent or cave. Role play camping trips, nomads, explorers.
● Set up an estate agent's office. Make a data bank to store information about types of houses, number of rooms, gardens, garages, prices, special features. Use local road maps to show positions of houses and recreational facilities. Role play telephone conversations between estate agent and clients.
● Talk with the children about neighbours: who lives in their street and what sorts of things do the children say to them? They could act out some of these conversations, and go on to put some examples into speech bubbles.

● **Make a houses and homes wall of words:**

● Make an alphabetical picture directory of jobs on a building site: architect, bricklayer, carpenter etc. Make up job descriptions. Add labelled diagrams, showing what various personnel might wear.

Maths

● Use plane shapes (circles, oblongs, triangles, squares) to make a variety of houses, e.g. bungalow, skyscraper, flat. Write labels showing the number and type of shapes used.
● Sort pictures of houses and homes onto a tree diagram: number of storeys or windows; type of roof or doors etc.

- Use carpet/lino tiles to estimate, then measure, areas of floors, desks, P.E. mats.
- Build houses from Dienes (or other structural apparatus). What is the value of each house?
- Survey children's door numbers. Put in order from lowest to highest. Sort into odd and even numbers. Find different number bonds, e.g. 21= 17+4. Use a calculator to halve/double/+10. How many different house numbers can be made from the figures 4, 3, 1?
- Calculate amounts of materials needed to make new furnishings for the doll or play house: tablecloths, curtains, carpeting.

Science
- Build 'blocks of flats' from different materials, e.g. paper cups, interlocking and wooden bricks, cotton reels, toilet roll tubes. Compare how stable they are. When/how do they collapse? Look at the size of the base and height. Was it a fair test?
- Make mud bricks in margarine tubs. Try adding pebbles, wood shavings, straw. Test for strength and durability.
- Make cardboard box rooms. Investigate floor and wall coverings (carpet, lino, tiles, wood, rush matting, wallpaper, vinyl etc). Decide which materials are best for bedrooms/bathrooms/kitchens (wear and tear, water resistance). Stack rooms to make houses/flats.
- Set up simple electrical circuits to light a room.

Humanities
- Use doll's house furniture, fuzzy felt, catalogue pictures or a cross-section baseboard of a house to arrange items in appropriate rooms. Think about space to move around easily, access to doors, windows, heaters etc.
- Use the 'Albert's House' computer program (BBC) to identify and explore rooms and their contents.
- Look at the similarities and differences between the children's houses, grandparents' houses (and possibly another historical period). Compare and contrast the living rooms (kitchen etc.) looking at changes in heating, lighting, furnishings, and domestic appliances. Label drawings and photographs to show your findings, and put them together as a reference book for the class library.

- Can the children draw a plan of their bedroom, their ideal room or a bedroom of the future?
- Look at pictures of houses around the world. Make a wall display showing how climate influences house design. Compile sets of pictures showing how houses are adapted to suit hot, rainy or cold places. Label features such as steep roofs, shutters, stilts and small windows.

Art and Craft/Design and Technology
- Use construction toys to make a play person's house with a window at the correct height, for it to see through.
- Look carefully at a range of house pictures to make a replica in damp sand or from construction toys.
- Cut out doors, windows, roofs, weather boarding etc. from old magazines and put some together to create your own collage houses.
- Design and make name/number plaques for a house or child's bedroom. Use stiff card, play dough, clay or stitched samplers. How can these be hung up?
- Look at colour/paint cards from DIY shops and mix paints to match these colours. Find collage materials and fabrics in the same shades.
- Discuss adaptations and household aids for the disabled: handrails on baths, ramps, special tin-openers etc. Draw 'before and after' pictures. (Contact agencies such as the Disabled Living Foundation and RNIB for information.)

Music
- Songs to learn: 'A House is a House For Me', 'How Many People Live in Your House?' 'I've Just Moved In' (*Tinderbox*, A & C Black); 'Building a House' (*Silly Aunt Sally*, Ward Lock Educational).
- Take household objects and try playing them in different ways (scrape, bang, blow). How many different sounds can you make with a metal teapot, saucepans, wooden spoons, an old cake tin, beakers, bowls or a kettle's whistle ?
- Make building site sounds. Use a xylophone/glockenspiel for climbing up and down ladders step by step, or walking along planks (beats stay on one note). How can you make the sounds of hammers tapping, tiles clinking, saws scraping or rubble sliding down a chute into a skip? Practise the sounds individually then put them together over a cement mixer drone.

Further activities from the book
- Research animal homes and build one from construction toys or junk materials to fit a soft toy or toy farm animal.
- **Play knock-down games to practise number skills.** Use empty drink cans and plastic bottles as skittles/coconut shies.

- Based on what went wrong with Mr and Mrs Brick's houses, devise a 'spot the deliberate mistakes' house game. Use fuzzy felt, card shapes etc. to make your own 'faulty houses'. Can a partner spot what's wrong and show how to put it right?
- Cut out faces from magazines and design frames for them. Invent names for the characters and display as a family portrait gallery.
- Think of names for other 'Happy Families' people with a houses and homes theme, e.g. the Paint family; Master Wood the Carpenter. You could make them into a set of cards to play a game of Happy Families.
- Find, adapt or design a container to prevent apples (oranges, cabbages) from being knocked off shelves.

Machines and Inventions

Make a model of one of Nina's machines

NINA'S MACHINES, Peter Firmin (Collins Young Lions)
The Mice and the Clockwork Bus, Rodney Peppe. **Robot,** Jan Pienkowski.
A Robot named Chip, Philippe Dupasquier. **Design a Pram,** Anne Fine.

Collections

Tools and machines which help us in school: calculator, tape recorder, clock, balances, pencil sharpener. Defunct machines for children to play with to see how they work. Bicycle pump, egg whisk, iron, toaster, typewriter, tin opener. Technic Lego and cog board. Any model toys or mechanical gadgets the children may have at home.

Starters

Discuss the children's ideas about what machines are - must they always be big, complicated and noisy? Compare their ideas with classroom machines - stapler, hole punch, clock, keyboard. Establish that a machine helps us to do a job more easily. Sort into categories, e.g. time machines; music machines, blowing machines (fan, hairdrier). Look at simple inventions the children may be wearing - zips, buckles, Velcro. Identify and display machines vocabulary: cogs, levers, wheels, push, pull, lift. Invite community members in to talk about machines they use - mechanics, computer programmers etc. Arrange an outside visit to see machines in action.

English

- Make a list of machine noises - clatter, rattle, click, clack. Practise saying them rhythmically. Put some together as a machine poem. Make the machine begin quietly and get noisier, or start slowly and gather speed.
- If you could only afford to buy one machine for your mum, dad, or a friend, which one would it be? How would it help them with what they like doing best?

- Think of jobs you hate doing - cleaning shoes, washing up. Draw a picture sequence, (or make a flow-chart program) for a robot to do the job instead.
- Look at a simple machine like a manual can opener. Describe its appearance, how it works and what it's for. Present in the form of a riddle.
- Give the children a short piece of text written on a 'faulty' typewriter. Make deliberate typing errors, spelling mistakes, misplace capitals, miss out full-stops or initial letters etc. Children 'proof read' the text, putting in the corrections.
- Imagine a machine getting out of control, e.g. a vacuum cleaner in suction overdrive. What would happen to wigs, rugs, house plants or small creatures? Put the machine at the centre, and around it show pictures with exclamatory speech bubbles describing the events.

Maths
- Using pictures of machines or real objects, how many solid shapes can the children spot? Match to your own collection of solid shapes and record what you find.
- **Use sticks or paper strips to show how each calculator number is made up.** Make a chart showing how many strips are needed for each figure. Is there any number pattern?

- **Use function machines**

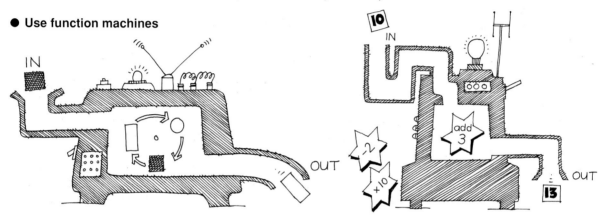

- Ask the children to make robots. Everyone must use 20 multi-link bricks. Are any of the robots the same? How many different ones have they made?
- Survey machines used at home. How many are found in the bedroom/bathroom, kitchen, living room? Are any found in more than one room? Which power source is most common?
- Given two paper circles of the same size, make one into a long spiral and the other into a short spiral (like a screw). How did you do it? Compare ideas with a friend.
- Draw symmetrical robots. Draw half a robot on squared paper (along a line of symmetry). Can a partner draw the matching half?

Science
- Talk about the properties of machines and people, looking for the things which are the same/different. Which have plastic/metal parts, need sleep, grow, make noises? Display on a Venn diagram.
- Explore how gears/cogs work. Use commercial cog boards or Technic Lego to arrange cogs in different patterns. Rotate one cog - what effect does it have on the others? Do they all move in the same direction/at the same speed?
- Do machines really save time? Choose a recipe which involves whisking - fresh banana milk shake, pancake batter or egg whites. Give the children a selection of beaters: electric/hand whisk, two forks, wooden spoon. Time which beater does the job quickest. Compare and interpret results.
- Find out about the power sources of inventions. Which use electricity, water, wind, sun etc? Label pictures and put your findings into a power resource pack for younger children. Alternatively, use pictures or real objects and label as part of a hands-on display.
- **Use cotton reels and elastic bands to show how belt-driven wheels work.**

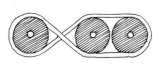 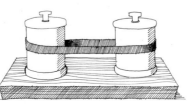 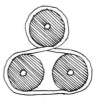

Humanities

- Go out on a local walk to find out about machines the children pass on the way to school. Take photographs/drawings, e.g. telephone box, bubble gum machine, cash dispenser. Where are machines sited and what are they used for? Make a 'Machines Around Us' display of your observations. You could use the same approach for a 'machines spot' in specific locations, e.g. school office, swimming pool, supermarket.
- Take a range of household objects (or use your machines display) and draw different views of them - side, top, plan. Play a game of matching the view to the real object.
- Look at a range of machines familiar to the children (cookers, washing machines etc). Find/draw pictures or artefacts of earlier versions of these machines. Label and place them in time order (now and then).
- Make a big book of inventors. Find out about, e.g., Jethro Tull, Richard Arkwright, Marconi and their famous inventions. Think how to arrange the book - chronological or alphabetical order; types of machines.

Art and Craft/Design and Technology

- Use a sewing machine to make a simple robot hand puppet. Decorate with shiny objects, e.g. sequins, buttons, foil.
- Take imprints of cogs, screws, bolts etc. in clay or play dough tiles. Mount the circular/square tiles together as a large wall 'machine'.
- Using junk materials, make a robot that has a simple moving part, e.g. dials, control knobs that turn, levers, belt-driven wheels.
- Take offset prints: ink up some metal objects or simple machines (nail, staple, scissors). Roll a printing roller over it, so the ink is on the roller. Transfer the print by rolling over a piece of clean paper. Arrange the prints - embellish with inks or felt-tip pens to make machine designs.
- Make a simple device to sort different sized cogs (screws, bolts, nails), or to sort nails from washers.
- Look at Heath Robinson pictures and use the ideas to design your own crazy invention, e.g. something to wash you at bath time; something for a toddler to eat spaghetti hoops without getting into a mess.

Music

- Sing 'Wheels Keep Turning' (*Apusskidu*, A & C Black). Choose percussion instruments to fit the sounds of levers, pistons, motors and wheels (guiro, castanets, cabasa, kokiriko, claves) and introduce them as they occur in the story.
- Talk about machine sounds you might hear in different parts of the house: washing machine, switches, cisterns flushing. Explore different ways of making the sounds using voice, body sounds and instruments. **Put ideas together in the form of a simple picture score.** Groups make their sounds as the conductor runs the pointer from left to right along the 'score'.

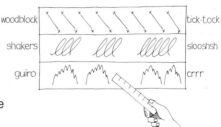

- Look at songs, poems and musical activities in the 'Machines' section of *Topic Anthologies 1* (J. Gilbert, OUP). Sing 'Magic Machine' (*Silly Aunt Sally,* A & C Black).

Further activities from the book

- Look at and discuss the sounds and movements that might fit one of Nina's machines. In groups, make body actions (stretching up and down, elbows in and out) and vocal sounds (clip, clop, splish) to complement her invention.
- Design and make a desk tidy for Nina. Will it fit inside a drawer, or stand on a work surface?
- Look carefully at the illustrations for clues about what Nina's Italian town was like. Find pictures of contemporary Italian villages and towns to compare and contrast. Which one is most like Nina's?
- If Nina decided to apply as an apprentice inventor in Orlando's workshop, instead of being the cleaner, how could she persuade him that she could do the job as well as the boys? Brainstorm and act out some ideas.
- Nina's bicycle was called the 'foot powered riding machine'. Make up similarly convoluted names for an electric guitar, garden sprinkler etc.

Celebrations

SEASONS OF SPLENDOUR, Madhur Jaffrey (Puffin)
Nini at Carnival, Errol Lloyd. **Maisie Middleton at the Wedding,** Nita Sowter.
Alfie gives a hand, Shirley Hughes.

Collections

Special occasion cards and wrapping papers: birthday, wedding, coming of age, retirement, anniversaries, Divali, Eid, Christmas, Hanukkah etc. Objects and photographs associated with special events the children have been involved in: carnival clothes, lucky red envelopes (for Chinese New Year), special foods. Commemorative stamps and posters for anniversaries of famous writers, artists, musicians and explorers.

Starters

Starting from the children's own experiences, discuss why and how we celebrate - parties, galas, festivals and ceremonies to mark special days and memories. Distinguish between personal celebrations (birthdays, anniversaries etc.) and those shared by the wider community (school events, feasts, festivals, jubilees). Make a large wall chart/calendar of these and decorate with a border of celebrations words (see English). Discuss: what's special about your festival; what do you enjoy about other people's celebrations; why do we exchange gifts at special times? Be sensitive - all cultures have their own way of celebrating. Invite members of particular faiths to talk to the children about how and why they celebrate.

English

● Use a photograph/drawing of celebrations the children have been involved in to describe: who's there, what is being celebrated, where is it taking place? You could make a tape and play a game of matching the descriptions to the pictures.

● Brainstorm words associated with celebrations (fun, happy, special etc). Include the names of celebrations and festivals, and associated signs and symbols. Make a banner of the word CELEBRATION.

● Sit in a circle and mime opening a present the children have received (or would like to receive). Can others guess what it is?
● Look at the words inside celebrations and greetings cards. Get the children to invent some of their own.
● Ask the children to select the perfect present for someone they know well. Discuss their reasons for choosing it. Older children could make a shopping suggestions list, or think of presents for well-known comic/story book characters.
● Compile a class 'party book' which gives suggestions for games to play, special foods to eat, songs to sing, decorations to make. Include a selection of cut-out pictures, children's drawings and instructions.

Maths

● Sort greetings cards by: size, with/without borders, picture/pattern on the front, type of greeting.
● Collect data to make a birthday graph. Interpret the information: how many children have a birthday this month, last month, next month - any months with no birthdays at all?

Illustrate one of the festivals celebrated in *Seasons of Splendour*

● How many different kinds of party sandwiches can be made with: brown/white bread and three fillings (cheese, Marmite, tomato)?

● **How many different oblong-shaped candles can be made with 12 pegs in a peg board (or cubes in a tray)?**

● Make some symmetrical designs using a cube tray, squared or dotty paper - using a mirror on an axis of symmetry to check.
● Make a probability line with the words: impossible, possible, likely, certain. Draw/find pictures of food, presents etc. under the appropriate word, e.g. food I definitely won't have/am likely to have.
● Find the birth dates of famous musicians, artists, local 'celebrities' - when will their centenary be? Use a symbol on a calendar to mark any that will be celebrated this year.

Science
● Identify a range of small 'presents' through different types of wrappings. Try feeling through rigid/soft boxes, tissue, cartridge, newspaper, soft plastic. Do any other senses, besides touch, help in the identification?
● Collect examples or make a list of the children's favourite party foods. Sort by: sweet/savoury, meat/vegetable, cooked or not. Display sets as party food labels or place markers.
● Which materials would be most suitable for a party tablecloth? Devise a fair test to find which materials: resist spilled juice (stays on top); soak it up; let it go right through.
● Investigate how best to send a fragile present through the post. Think about the outside container and the inside packaging. Why are tissue, polystyrene chippings and newspaper often used? Test these and other materials by wrapping up some chalks.

Humanities
● Take a celebration (like a birthday) and compare the similarities and differences for you, your father, grandma, great grandma. Look at: food eaten, clothes worn, games played, guests. Display the information on four different cake outlines arranged in time order.
● Find out about local buildings and venues which are (or have been) used for celebrations - reception

halls, places of worship, parks and playing fields for fetes and jubilees etc. Take photographs/drawings to display who goes there, when and why.
- Talk about familiar school celebrations. Look at entries in the school log book to make a calendar/timeline showing when similiar events took place. Does the log record any other information, e.g. weather, special guests, unexpected happenings?
- Look at commemorative stamps, mugs, tins, plates etc. Place the objects and pictures in a labelled timeline.
- Consider one type of celebration - birthday, wedding, new year - and compare/contrast how it is marked by various peoples. Pin all the ideas on to, e.g., an old wedding dress or baby's shawl.

Art and Craft/Design and Technology
- Make celebration wrapping paper for someone special to the children. Impress a simple pattern on a printing block (old Plasticine, press print). Fold the printing paper into squares or oblongs to help place the prints.
- Look at how headgear, face paints and masks are used in celebrations. Model your own for a class celebration.
- Design and make a theme party pack - hats, party bags, place-name labels - make sure they all reflect the theme.
- Design a commemorative stamp for the school jubilee or famous local personality.

Music
- Sing and play some of the songs and activities in *Festivals* (J. Gilbert, OUP).
- You will find a good variety of other celebration songs in *Mango Spice, Harlequin, Tinderbox* (all A & C Black).
- Listen to a wide range of celebratory music (carnival - calypso, steel band, Chinese lion dance, classical Indian music). Encourage the children to bring in some of their own music. Is all celebration music happy and bright?
- Make up some music for a party game - either like musical bumps with lots of stops and starts (how do the instrumentalists agree on stop/start signals?) or, a game where children have to match an instrument to a particular movement, e.g. skip every time a triangle is played, walk to the drum, freeze when you hear the tambourine.

Further activities from the book
- Children could make collage pictures of themselves to add to a frieze celebrating Rama and Sita's homecoming. Make the welcoming lights and garland flowers (in reds and yellows) central to the art work. Try making vibrant 2D and 3D candles (thick wax crayon, wax resist, metallic papers, braid, sequins, foil, glitter and coloured paper pieces).
- Make a 'welcome home' banner - how many different ways of writing this greeting can the children include on their banner?
- Design and make Divali cards using either rangoli or mendhi patterns. Try using powder paint, chalk, coloured grains, pasta or seeds. Draw round hands and fill in with detailed geometric motifs or characters from handwriting scripts to make mendhi patterns (as on henna-painted hands).
- Focus on the story-telling tradition by asking the children to retell one of the stories from the book. Use a flannel board or hand/shadow puppets to help.
- Look through the book and plot on a calendar the major celebrations of the Hindu year.
- Plan a celebratory meal. Research appropriate sweetmeats and special foods for a Divali feast. **Give the menu a border of traditional Indian patterns.**

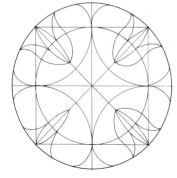  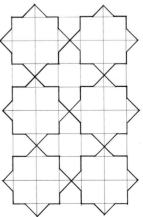

Food

THE PERFECT HAMBURGER, Alexander McCall Smith (Young Puffin)
Mrs Wobble the Waitress, A. and J. Ahlberg. **Teddy Bears Eat Out,** Susanna Gretz/A.Sage.
Mrs Pig's Bulk Buy, Mary Rayner. **Leon's Lucky Lunch Break,** Mary Hoffman.

Collections
Modern, old and replica food tins, packaging and carrier bags. Cooking utensils. Containers to carry food home in from the shops (baskets, trollies, boxes). Take-away cartons from fast food outlets. Old and new recipe books. Menus from different types of restaurant (vegetarian, fast food, Chinese).

Starters
Be sensitive towards a range of dietary views. Capitalise on the multi-cultural aspect of food in your discussions. What do the children think is the best/worst part about cooking? Talk about food as a source of energy. On cards, show the names of meals taken at different times of the day. Play sequence games with them. Look together at how recipe books are arranged:- starters, main courses, sweets, contents/index and photographs. What staple foods are eaten as part of the main meal (potatoes, rice, pasta)? Make an alphabetical list of cooking methods (bake, fry, roast etc). Talk about the differences between eating out/at home. What do the children know about convenience foods?

English/Role Play
● Set up a café. Vote on the name which best reflects the type of food it serves. Will it have an international flavour or is it a fish and chip/fast food café? What staff will you need (waiter, cook, kitchen porter)? Make menus, bills, logos, place mats. Promote a 'grand opening' - cut the ribbon, serve the first meal.
● Make a class recipe book with a theme - drinks, picnic or party food. Add a contents, index and glossary of cooking terms. Invite children to bring favourite recipes from home to add to the book.
● Compile a list of the children's favourite snacks, e.g. a sandwich or beans on toast. Make a picture flow chart to show how it's made. Give an idea of quantities, utensils needed, cooking times.
● Plan a surprise lunch for someone you know well. Make a list of all the things you need to buy, prepare and do. Or plan a menu for a tasty meal to tempt the dragon away from gobbling up a princess.
● Collect some names of dishes like 'hot dog', 'cottage pie', 'cup cakes'. Make a picture showing what one of these might look like - literally. Find out, or imagine how the dishes got their names.

Maths

- Take a lump of play dough and a range of different sized/shaped cutters. How many 'biscuits' can be cut out? Look at size of cutter, how cuts are arranged, thickness of dough.
- Use clock faces to show the sequence of children's meal times. How much time each day is spent eating? Include snack times, playtime breaks, after school nibbles.
- How many drinks can be made from a bottle of squash? Estimate. Test (dilution/size of cup).
- Make a graph of children's favourite/most loathed foods.
- Explore a tin/packet. Measure its height, depth, perimeter, circumference, weight. How many would fit on a shelf 1m long, or pack in a carton? How many for £1? What is its net?
- Record types of food eaten for school meals or packed lunches - meat, fruit, vegetables, grain, dairy products. At the end of the week, look at the totals under each type of food. What could this usefully tell us about the kind of diet we have?
- **Use picture menus to work out the cost of meals.**

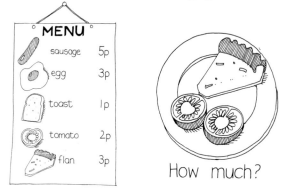

- Fill a lunch box. You are allowed to choose three things each day from this list: sandwiches, crisps, fruit, biscuits or yoghurt. Can you make up a different lunch box for every day of the week?

Science

- Which foods are eaten raw and which are cooked? Cut out pictures of food and put into sets. How can you show foods which can be eaten either way?
- Identify flavours of sweets/crisps. Try by smell alone, then taste, then taste while holding nose. How easy was it to tell? Chart your findings.
- How is food cooked at home? Collect pictures of ovens, toasters, microwaves, slow cookers, barbecues. Label their energy sources (electric, gas, solid fuel) and display beside a cooking safety poster.
- Use the traffic light principle to help children to identify the foods they can eat freely, and those which should be eaten in moderation. Show these as paper plate collages of balanced meals.
- What happens if food is left uncovered? Keep a diary of the changes over time. Wash hands!

Humanities

- Find out about local eating places. Where are the restaurants and take-aways? What can you eat there? **Display the information on a map or circle diagram.** Older children could use the Yellow Pages to extend the map or make up a quiz. Where can you get Chinese/Greek food? Can you buy fish and chips at 8 p.m. on Wednesdays?

- How were foods preserved before fridges? Survey a local food shop. Start with fresh peas or potatoes - can you get them frozen, tinned, bottled, dried? Chart your findings.
- Research national dishes, e.g. bortsch, quiche, goulash. Make models of the food. Include a flag place-mat of their country of origin. Do the same with regional dishes: Cornish pastie, Yorkshire parkin.
- Find out about rationing. Which foods were available? Look at quantities allowed for a week. What kinds of substitutes were used? Display by comparing a child's lunch box with that of 40 years ago.

Art and Craft/Design and Technology
- Use fruit and vegetables to print. Cut different cross sections (circle, ellipse) through the vegetable to get a range of shapes and sizes. Make regular patterns (rows and columns, reflection, rotation). Use as a border for a menu card, carrier bag or a coving frieze for a café.
- Make table decorations for a café, e.g. flowers in vases, floating candles.

- Make a basket, carrier or shopping trolley to carry a specific load - 2 cereal packets, 4 apples etc.
- Make composite food advertisements from magazine pictures. Alternatively, devise an advertisement for a product that couldn't possibly sell! Juxtapose things such as a plate of scampi and chips with tummy ache pills; ice cream and rotten teeth; a rodent nibbling the Edam.
- Design a label for a tin. Make sure it can be read from the front. Think about clear, eye-catching lettering. How could this be adapted for somebody with poor eyesight?

Music
- Say 'favourite foods' words in strong rhythmic patterns. You say and clap the rhythm - beefburger - and children echo the pattern. Find other food words with the same pattern (fish finger, cheese toastie). Try other rhythm groups: apple pie, fish and chips, jelly beans; or tea, soup, jam. Play spot the odd one out games - egg and bacon, plums and custard...toast.
- Learn 'The Super-Supper March' (*Apusskidu*, A & C Black). Substitute 'frittered flum' etc. for your own imaginary dishes.
- Sing: 'Sticky Side Down', 'Pepper Song' (*Silly Aunt Sally,* Ward Lock Educational); 'Magical Food' (*The Music Box Songbook,* BBC); Songs from the food theme in *Mango Spice* (A & C Black).

Further activities from the book
- Write a senses poem describing a hamburger or other favourite food. Each sense will be one line of the poem. Each line only has one or two words, except the last one which is a short phrase summing up either the food or the child's feelings about it. (See photograph.)
- Use Plasticine or play dough to make a burger and share it fairly between 2 (4,8,3,6,5) people. Which is hardest/easiest? How would you share a satsuma, chocolate bar, packet of assorted biscuits?
- Make a condiment tray for Mr Borthwick's cafe. Can you make the tray revolve?
- Look at different types of burger, e.g. beef, ham, bean. Devise a completely new type of burger. Give it a name. List ingredients and offer serving suggestions.
- Take one or two pinches from each of Mr. Borthwick's tins (green, brown, black). How many combinations will you try out before Joe has the perfect spice additions?
- Research herbs and spices. Display findings by adding name and picture labels to spice jars. Show the country of origin.

Pets

THE BATTLE OF BUBBLE AND SQUEAK, Philippa Pearce (Puffin)
Mog and the Baby, Judith Kerr. **Sam's Cat,** Sarah Garland.
John Brown, Rose and the Midnight Cat, Jenny Wagner. **Fred,** Posy Simmonds.

Collections
Cages, perches, hutches and carrying containers for a range of pets. Collars, leads, grooming tools, identification tags, and pet toys such as rubber bones and hamster wheels. Pet foods. RSPCA posters and leaflets, vet appointment cards, pedigrees. Photographs of children with their pets. Magazine pictures. A class pet (if school guidelines allow), or pets brought in specially for the day.

Starters
Be sensitive to differing attitudes towards pets within ethnic groups. What is a pet? Group animals into domestic (pets, farm animals) and wild. Talk about and make a check list of a pet's basic needs (warmth, shelter, food, exercise, affection). Relate to the children's needs - is there anything we need which pets do not? Compare pet/human skeleton pictures or models. How else are pets the same/different (skin, fur, toes, claws etc)? Find out about working animals, e.g. guide/police/sheep dogs. Visits: sheep dog trials, pigeon club, vets, cattery.

English
● Recount stories about some of the funny things the children's pets do (or talk about characters like Tom and Jerry, Gnasher and Gnipper). Make a cartoon strip showing either a pet's antics or a sequel to an existing cartoon. What usually happens in their adventures?
● Make up a 'pets' poem starting: ' My dog likes to —- (curl up on my lap, munch my jeans —-).'
● Make a list, or draw pictures of the front covers of other stories/poems featuring pets. Feature favourites in an 'Our book of the week' display.
● Make up riddles to describe pets. Include: appearance, movement, noises, one special thing they love doing.
● Talk about the responsibilities and pleasures of having pets. Advantages might include: fun to play with; makes you feel safe; catches mice. Disadvantages: scratching furniture, expensive, smelly. Cut out pet silhouette shapes (use one colour for pros and one for cons) and use to display their ideas.
● Arrange for someone to bring a pet into school for the day. Discuss travel arrangements and recap on the animal's basic needs. Write a set of instructions (or use pictures and short captions) for somebody to look after the animal, e.g. first-time owners or holiday 'pet sitters'. Design and write information leaflets about how to care for particular pets.
● What might some everyday objects look like from a gerbil's eye view? What is it like to see everything through bars, or to approach a table leg? Display the children's ideas as pictures and speech bubbles ('Good gracious me' etc).

Maths
● Survey children's pets. Make a mapping diagram matching children to their pets. Use this information to make a picture graph of the different types of pets. Which is the most popular pet? How many cats/dogs are there? How many more cats than dogs/gerbils? Find the total number of pets.
● Use Carroll diagrams to sort dog biscuits/bird grain by shape, pattern, colour and size.
● Make a large, wall decision tree to sort pets in different ways. Children sort by answering questions like: does it have fur, feathers, scales, four legs? Does it eat meat? Is it bigger than a box of cereal? Make pictures of pets (collage, paint or draw) and place in the appropriate position on the tree. Use this as an interactive display - how many different ways can the children sort pets using different questions?
● Make a timetable for a pet. Find out about feeding times, exercise, grooming, visits to vet, special events.
● Find out how much a pet eats in a day/week/month. How much would this cost? Is there a relationship between the pet's size and how much it eats? Price other pet requirements: bedding, health care, toys.

We have designed and made a travel box for Bubbles.

Science

● **Plant gerbil or budgie food** in compost to discover which seeds and grain it contains.

● Look closely at paw/claw prints made in wet sand or mud. Carefully draw the imprint. Compare and contrast animal prints with children's feet (number of toes, shape, claws, pads).

● Find out about animal senses. Talk about the similarities and differences between children's/pets' senses. What are cats' whiskers for? Why do gerbils sniff? What is special about a rabbit's ears? Display on a labelled picture of the pet showing special senses and use.

● Make a pets' data base. Give headings such as: name of owner, type of pet, measurements, age, favourite foods, special requirements.

● Given a choice, what do pets prefer to eat? Make available piles of different types of seeds or green stuffs. Record the order in which foods were taken, amounts, and those left untouched. Make a picture tally chart of your observations. Be reasonable in your choices. Do not offer foods which may be harmful.

Humanities

● Use a range of resource materials to look for evidence that pets and people have co-existed throughout the ages. Look at pictures of ancient friezes, clay pots, boxes, jewellery, tapestries. Did they have the same pets as we have now? How might people in the past have felt about their pets? Did pets have another significance (religious/work)? Put pictures, and real objects, in order on a timeline.

● Look at the provision for dogs in your locality. Note features like: signs prohibiting/allowing dogs, dog toilets, buildings which do/do not allow dogs. Why are they there? Draw or make a simple model showing what already exists, and other things you'd like to have.

● What did pets eat before supermarkets sold food in tins and packets? Make a display showing the pet surrounded by labels and packets of food they eat now. Do the same for what they might have eaten before convenience foods.

● Look at, and discuss, television and magazine advertisements featuring pets (Dulux dog, Andrex puppy etc). Which products are they promoting? Look at older advertisements (tins and labels, old journals). Are they the same/different? Which advertisement would you put your pet in?

Art and Craft/Design and Technology

● Look at different ways pets have been shown in book illustrations. Find a range of techniques used: water colour, pen and ink, collage. Choose one of these techniques and portray a pet in the same way.

● Design and make a suitable container to transport a pet from home to school. Think about safety, space, comfort, warmth and whether or not it likes to see out. Include a door flap that opens and closes securely. (See photograph.)

● Make a headdress/mask (or use face paints) to dress up as a favourite pet. Think carefully about shape and placement of ears, eyes, whiskers, and facial expression.

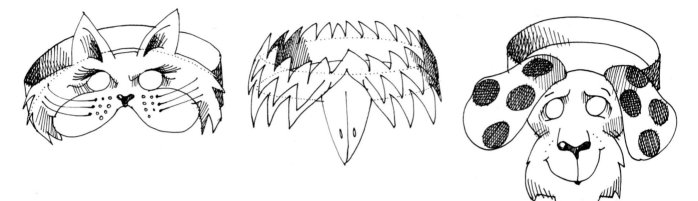

● Look carefully at, then make, a pet's toy that moves: swinging perch, turning wheels, rocking/weighted toys.

Music
● Sing 'Catastrophe', 'Has anyone here got a puppy?' (*Silly Aunt Sally,* Ward Lock Educational); 'My Cat and I' (*Birds and Beasts,* A & C Black); 'Jennifer's Rabbit' (*Tinderbox,* A & C Black).
● Design and make a suitable container to transport a pet from home to school. Think about safety, space, comfort, warmth and whether or not it likes to see out. Include a door flap that opens and closes securely. Play a listening game. Decide on some vocal sounds associated with pets (mouse squeak, cat miaow, rabbit snuffle). Make these sounds and add simple movements, e.g. cats washing, mouse's twitching nose. Divide the children into three groups. Each group has a leader who will play an instrument (finger cymbals for mouse, shakers, for rabbit, xylophone for cat). Leaders stand together and every time they play their instrument the rest of the group joins in with the pet sound and movement. As soon as the group's instrument stops playing, those dancers freeze.

Further activities from the book
● Think of words that go together like Bubble and Squeak. What could you call another pair of gerbils - Bangers and Mash, Thunder and Lightning? Try pairs of opposites: high/low, full/empty, sweet/sour.
● Use junk materials to devise tunnels, mazes and obstacle courses for Bubble and Squeak to enjoy.
● Make some sugar mice like the ones Dad brought home. Or find recipes for biscuits and cakes to make and decorate into animal shapes.
● Play a game of Bubble and Squeak. Children take turns to say a number each, as they count up in sequence around a circle. If their number contains a 0 they must 'squeak' instead. Say 'bubble' if the number has a three in it. For example, 1,2, bubble, 4,5,6,7,8,9, squeak, 11. Adapt to practise odd/even numbers, patterns of 2, 3, 5, 10 etc.
● Make pet-for-sale notices. Use persuasive words to 'sell' your pet's best qualities. How can the advert be made to stand out on a class noticeboard - lettering, borders, decoration?

Dark

THE OWL WHO WAS AFRAID OF THE DARK, Jill Tomlinson (Mammoth, Methuen)
One Moonlit Night, Ronda & David Armitage. **Can't you sleep, Little Bear?** Martin Waddell
A Dark, Dark Tale, Ruth Brown. **Mog in the Dark,** Judith Kerr.

Collections

Night wear, comforters, soft toys in bed. Lamps, torches, candles, electric night-lights, clocks. Pictures, toys and models of: night creatures (owl, hedgehog, fox, etc), night-time workers, silhouettes. Paintings by famous artists, e.g. Van Gogh's 'Starry Night'.

Starters

Talk about and demonstrate how we have light and dark; day and night. What do the children know about the moon - when can they see it? Talk about night time rituals (getting ready for bed, closing the curtains, bedtime stories). Encourage the children to voice their own feelings about the dark - what do they like/dislike about it? Display dark/light vocabulary on sun and moon shapes.

English

● Act out the worried child and the reassuring older person. Begin the scenario with 'On a dark night I heard ...(squeak)'. Ask, 'What's that noise .... who's that?' Encourage the children to give responses like: 'It's only Hetty the Hamster'. Extend by making a three-picture sequence: 'What I heard', 'What I thought it was', 'What it really was'.

● Talk about dreams and ask the children to retell some. You could display their ideas in wonderful/scary dream bubbles. Older children could go on to invent some day dreams for nocturnal animals.

- Compile a comforting bed-time tape for yourself or to help parents/minders with a younger sibling. You could include: favourite stories or rhymes; soothing music and lullabies.
- Display 'IGHT' words on star shapes (bright, night, fright, light). Choose one (or more) of the words and take turns to use it in a 'dark sentence'.

Maths
- Make a simple picture sequence of the children's day (getting up, school, home, bed). Or, show a sequence of what they do at different clock times, e.g. 8, 9, 12, 3, 5, 7 o'clock.
- How many different star patterns can you make using triangular Polydrons (or card shapes)? Can the children draw their star shapes on triangular paper?
- **Complete the 'dark' grids.**

- Work out how long the children spend sleeping each day/week. Show as a pie chart (like a sun or full moon). Or, make a bar chart with clock faces showing bedtimes - who goes to bed before/after seven o'clock?
- Cut out some star shapes and number them 1-9. Any three stars can 'shoot' and disappear at the same time. What is the highest/lowest star total which can disappear? Record these and any other totals you can make.

Science
- Investigate torches. Let the children look inside to consider how they work. Look at how the batteries are placed and what happens when the children try the torch without them. Experiment with different battery arrangements, and draw simple pictures to show when the torch is lit up.
- What sources of night-time lighting can the children tell you about (street lights, moonlight, headlights)? Talk about reflectors, Cat's-eyes, luminous clothing. Take a street scene and make day and night time versions, showing a range of lights, shadows, silhouettes etc.
- Devise a fair test to investigate which colours show up in the dark. Try clothing or toy cars in front of different coloured backgrounds.
- Make a sketch book of nocturnal animals, showing sizes and habitats. The children could go on to make symbols to show: animals they have seen themselves; those that also come out during the day; what they eat (herbivore/carnivore).
- Think about the difference between stars and planets. Find out about constellations (Orion, the Great Hunter; Sirius, the Dog Star) and display some of these on a star map - or make up your own dot-to-dot star patterns.

Humanities
- Talk and find out about the sorts of jobs which have to be done while others sleep (hospital care, mail sorting, security etc). Which jobs are carried out only at night, only during the day, or during both day and night? Display your findings using Venn or mapping diagrams. (See photograph.)
- What did we use before electric lights? Make a collection of pictures to show a range of lighting. Which ones do we still use today? Display the 'then' pictures on a candle outline and the 'now' pictures on an electric lamp shape. Match the ones used both then and now.

- How have people measured time? Look at the development from shadows, water clocks, sun dials, through to pendulum clocks and digital watch displays. Show the progression by putting pictures and dates on a candle-shaped timeline.
- Find the opening and closing times of shops and services in your locality - corner shop/supermarket, library, bus station etc. Write night shops/services on dark mounts and display on the 'night side' of a clock face. Do the reverse for daytime services.

Art and Craft/Design and Technology
- Make sgraffito pictures (wax and scratch) of night-time creatures, moon monsters or things that go bump in the night.
- Make night-life shadow puppets.

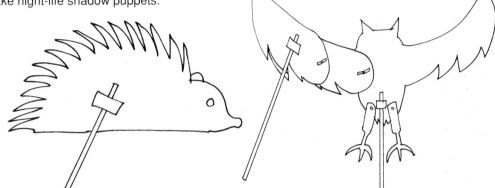

- Make model fireworks focusing on the shape sparks make as they fall. Compare the fountain firework with sparklers, which explode from the centre, and the caterpillar shapes of jumping jacks.
- Use an overhead projector to cast shadows of different objects. Use these silhouette shapes to create a night skyline. Mount on a colour wash of blues, greys and mauves.
- Make a nocturnal animal, such as an owl or hedgehog, with moving eyes. Use simple card strips, with eyes drawn on them, which can be moved sideways or up and down. Experiment with ways of making the eyes open and close either fully or half way.
- Make a cradle that rocks for a Lego/soft toy; or a bunk bed with a ladder.

Music
- Learn some lullabies from *The Music Box Song Book* (BBC): 'Sleep, Sleep, Sleep', 'Manx Lullaby', 'A Highland Lullaby'. Make steady, rocking and swaying movements as you sing. From the 'Cradle Song' (in the same collection), one group could whisper 'hush, hush', throughout the song as others hum/sing. Then add a chime bar accompaniment (bars D & F), tapping out the word rhythm, 'stars, stars', or 'go to sleep'.
- 'The Owl Who was Afraid of the Dark' (*Sing A Story*, A & C Black) retells the story of Plop in the song.
- More rousing theme songs: 'Ten in the Bed', 'Bananas in Pyjamas' (*Apusskidu*, A & C Black); 'Things That Go Bump In The Night' (*Phantasmagoria*, A & C Black) and 'Aiken Drum' (traditional).

Further activities from the book
- Make some clay/dough models of owls and other creatures mentioned in the book.
- Fill a pyjama or wash bag with night time items: tooth brush, tube of toothpaste, sponge, comb etc. Use it as a feely bag.
- Try some of Plop's landings: like a Catherine wheel; a roly-poly pudding; a shooting star. Try out alternative movements for other creatures, e.g. hedgehog, bat.
- Read out the contents list as a poem. The children can make their own 'Dark is' poem, thinking about what they say, feel and hear in the dark. This could be adapted to make a class poem. One stanza describes what the children don't like about the dark - ending with, 'I don't like it AT ALL', and one stanza describes all the good things ending with, 'Dark is SUPER'.
- Talk about manners and recall some the little old lady told Plop: 'I beg your pardon?' 'No Boasting' etc. Ask the children to suggest some other ways of being polite to each other in the classroom. List and display their ideas as a 'Good Manners' poster.
- Make a Christmas stocking or gift bag for Plop. Fill it up with his favourite foods and playthings: a toy grasshopper, sugar shrews, his own landing pad, an alarm clock, a book for his discoveries.

Sounds

PATRICK, Quentin Blake (Collins Picture Lions)
Peace at Last, Jill Murphy. **Trubloff,** John Burningham. **All Join in,** Quentin Blake.
The Emperor's Nightingale, H.C.Anderson (retold by S.Greenway).

Collections
A collection of 'sound makers' (musical instruments and everyday objects): wood blocks, drum, coconut shells, shakers, tambourine, recorder, bells, cymbals; metal teapot, sandpaper, yoghurt pots, tubes; beaters with hard and soft heads, wooden spoons, rulers, pencils and straws. Toys and other objects that make sounds. Radio, cassette, personal stereo.

Starters
Warn the children not to shout, make loud noises or poke anything down ears. Look at the shape and position of ears. Discuss what hearing is about (receiving messages, pleasant sounds, alarm signals). See and hear vibrations: put fingers on throats whilst singing, humming and shouting; watch what happens when you 'ping' a ruler. Sit still with eyes closed in the classroom (and/or outside) and listen to the sounds. Can the children sort them into, e.g., human; mechanical, information? Look at comic strips and poems and make a collection of sound words - Pow! Zap! Splash! Play Chinese whispers and miming games. Invite the school nurse in to talk about hearing tests.

English
● Make an 'animal sounds' book for a toddler. Illustrate and add simple captions: the cow goes moo; the duck goes quack etc. Try other themes, e.g. instruments, household sounds.
● Find some pictures of busy scenes, e.g. inside a supermarket or swimming pool. Can the children mime one of these situations while others guess where they are?
● Talk about quiet sounds. Make similes like: 'as quiet as a whisper to a friend', 'a feather falling'. Try some noisy similes.
● Think about the sounds of words. Do the children think some sound funny (rhubarb); fast (pop,zip); strong; beautiful (lapis lazuli)? **Make and illustrate collections of these words** (reflect their quality in the type of print used, decoration and shape, e.g. explosive bubbles, a meandering line).

ZIP   *lapis - lazuli*

● Make a five minute tape, for a children's radio programme. List the things you might include: a signature tune, linking jingles, retelling a story, songs/rhymes, a tongue twister or joke slot. Make a running order list.
● Talk about words that sound the same, but are spelt differently: hare/hair, knight/night, waist/waste. Some children can use dictionary skills to find alternative meanings. Make picture captions of the pairs of words - one showing appropriate use of the word, the other showing inappropriate use or confusion, e.g. 'My head is covered with ginger hares/hairs'.

Maths
● Sort sounds into those heard inside or outside the classroom - are any heard in both?
● Make a number song tape - start with the excellent collection in *Count With Me* (A & C Black).
● How many cassettes will fit into an old tissue box? Does it make a difference if they are laid flat or stacked on end? Try different boxes and compare your findings.

● **Find pairs of jingles that total the tambourine number.**

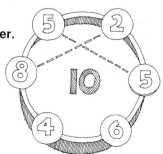

Instead of apples the trees began to grow pears, bananas, cakes, ice-creams and toast.

Help yourself!

Make a frieze showing the magical effects of Patrick's violin music

● Make a survey of the children's favourite school songs, records or pop stars.
● Take three different sized triangles or chime bars. If each is played once, how many different patterns can be played? Try more bars and tunes.
● Get the children to make you a reminder diary for tape recording school broadcasts (days of the week, starting and finishing times). How many 30 minute tapes will you need?
● How long is an audio tape? Use an old tape to look at how it is wound, estimate and then measure. What other things are coiled and can be unwound (tape measure, string, wool? (You could take small samples and wind them on to card circles.

Science
● Sort your collection of sound makers by exploring the different ways sounds can be made - shake, tap, pluck, scrape, blow. Can some children suggest/find out what was vibrating to produce the sound?
● Investigate ways to make a small sound louder. Try cupping hands around ears; making card ear trumpets, megaphones or a stethoscope (funnel and plastic tube). Discuss how and why they work.
● Investigate pitch by making xylophones or tubular bells. Fill some bottles with various levels of water, or suspend different lengths of copper piping/nails from a piece of dowelling. What can the children discover about the kinds of sounds they make? Can they order them in pitch from lowest to highest?
● Explore how far a sound travels. Drop a button onto a tin lid (or shake a bell), and devise a test to find out how far away the sound can still be heard. Does it make a difference if one ear is covered?
● Talk about who might need ear protectors and how sounds can be muffled. Devise tests like: listening to a sound with hands/hood covering the ears; making ear muffs (pads of cotton wool, newspaper, bubble plastic). What can be done to the sound maker itself to quieten it (turn down the volume, stand it on a different surface, surround it with materials)?

Humanities

- Make a picture map of the sounds associated with familiar local places: shopping centre, place of worship, library. What kinds of sounds are there (from bird calls to pneumatic drills)? Are some locations noisier than others?
- Where do the children think are the quietest/noisiest places around the school? Do they all agree on what constitutes 'noisy'? Do sound levels vary at different times of the day? Display the findings on a plan of the school - shade noisy areas (dark), through to lighter shading for quiet places.
- Look closely at a range of artefacts and pictures for evidence of musical instruments: Ancient Egyptian friezes; patterns on bowls and plates; prints. How are these the same/different from instruments the children know about now? Group them into families of sounds (string, wind, percussion). Or try matching an older instrument to one resembling a present day version (rebec/recorder, drums).
- Make a simple book of famous inventors and their sound machines - radio, telephone, phonograph.

Art and Craft/Design and Technology

- Listen to a short extract of music which suggests a strong feeling of movement, e.g. floating and curling or strong and spiky. Can the children translate the sounds into an abstract 'shape pattern' on paper?
- Make some simple musical instruments from junk materials, e.g. stretch a plastic bag 'skin' over a bin, card tube or tin. Experiment with other skins - balloons, paper, card, leather. Try making scrapers and shakers.
- **Make some pottery wind chimes** by cutting out some simple clay shapes to decorate with scratch patterns and paint. Make a hole in each shape to string together as a mobile.
- Design a quiet corner for the class. Discuss what this area is for: reading, thinking, or quiet activities. How can it be made to serve these purposes, and be cosy and welcoming? What can be done to encourage people not to interrupt?
- Design the picture sleeve for a tape, record or CD. Or, design and make a rack to hold six cassettes.

Music

- Tap out the rhythm of a favourite class song or nursery rhyme. Can the children recognise it without the tune?
- Sit the children in a circle and give them each an instrument. They take turns to make a sound on their instrument, but not until the previous sound has died away. At first you may want to start with instruments that all have long, ringing sounds (cymbal, triangle, chime bar).
- Listen to short musical extracts and try to identify how the sound is being produced (blow, scrape, hit), or to recognise an individual instrument. Try Britten's 'Young Person's Guide to the Orchestra'; Prokofiev's 'Peter and the Wolf', or pop music with guitar solos and drum breaks.
- Use an IT program such as 'Compose' (BBC) or 'Compose World' (Archimedes). Children select and arrange picture symbols to create their own musical compositions.

Further activities from the book

- Make a frieze showing Patrick leading the procession to town. Use this as a basis for maths activities such as: labelling position and ordinal numbers; ordering by size; counting in groups of 2, 5, 10.
- Make a musical accompaniment to the book, giving each of the characters their own special tune - invent other characters and tunes to add to Patrick's procession.
- Look at objects through coloured acetate. Observe and record the changes in colour - any surprises?
- Transform the plain to the spectacular! Make a printing block from old Plasticine. Take one print and leave it plain. Make a second print and embellish it vividly. Display the two prints next to each other.

- **Make a box and elastic band 'violin'.** Compare the different sounds made with longer, shorter, thinner, thicker bands and various shaped boxes. Can the children make a bridge for the violin using two pieces of wood? What happens to the sounds now?

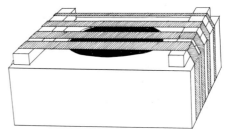

- Make your own second-hand stall and act out that part of the Patrick story. Or give the story a new twist, e.g. what might happen if the Tinker bought the clock?

Feet and Footwear

NOT SO FAST SONGOLOLO, Niki Daly (Picture Puffin)
Alfie's Feet, Shirley Hughes. **Mr Magnolia,** Quentin Blake. **The Sandal,** Tony Bradman.
The Shoemaker's Boy, Joan Aiken.

Collections
Footwear for different purposes and made from a range of materials: new and old shoes, trainers, walking boots, skates, slippers, skis, galoshes, support shoes for the disabled. Cleaning materials. Socks: long, short, patterned, plain, different materials. Shoe boxes and cartons, foot gauge, shoe horns, shoe last. Footwear advertising materials. Towel, talc, corn pads, verruca sock to show foot health care.

Starters
Talk about the different kinds of shoes the children are wearing: size, shape and design, colour, fastenings, materials (fabric, natural/man-made, shiny/dull) and decoration. Discuss socks and tights, concentrating on lengths, thickness, colours, similarities and differences. Investigate pairs of things. Compare and contrast left and right feet and shoes - how are they the same, or different? Can the children recall and recount a time when they had a different or special pair of shoes? Visit a local shoe shop or factory. Invite a shoe shop assistant or cobbler to talk to the children.

English/Role Play
● Talk about what the children have used their feet for so far today - walking, kicking a ball, climbing etc. (See photograph.) Brainstorm other uses of feet: playing sports, tip-toeing etc. Put these ideas into a cinquain poem (1-2-3-4-1 words in each line). Mount the poems on foot-shaped silhouettes.
● Create a shoe shop. Role play customer, assistant, window dresser. Think up a catchy name for the shop, e.g. 'Feet First', 'Stepping Out'. Make a simple foot gauge and some tiered display stands. Can all the shoes be seen? Try arranging shoes in groups: adult, child, sports/work, colours etc. Find or design price lists, receipt pads, sale and bargain notices, carrier bags. Make a poster to promote a new line of shoe.

- Using cut-out pictures and children's drawings, make a footwear catalogue. Each page has the shoe type and alternative names (plimsolls/pumps/trainers) as a heading. Under the picture list: special features, sizes available, price.
- Write the journey of a pair of shoes from the viewpoint of the shoes or the person wearing them, e.g. Farmer Fothergill's wellies, a jester's shoes, the children's plimsolls.
- Make a concertina book of foot sayings. Each page illustrates a different foot saying: 'best foot forward', 'two left feet', 'put your foot down', etc.

Maths
- Conduct a survey of shoe fastenings (Velcro, slip-on, zip, buckle, laces). Which is the most common fastening? Compare child/adult shoe fastenings.
- Estimate, then measure, distances in shoe lengths (heel-toe, paces, strides). Try using a toddler's or adult's shoe. Discuss and chart results.
- Explore the capacity of shoe boxes using non standard and standard units (1 box holds: 20 wooden bricks, 3 balls, 12 match boxes). How many shoe boxes fit into a large carton? What is the most efficient way to fill the carton?
- Draw round and cut out footprints. Use to display as a number line to count in twos, fives, tens (feet and toes). Explore these patterns using a 100 square, cube 'steps' or the constant facility on a calculator (10 + = = =).
- How many different ways can laces be tied using 4, 6, 8 holes?

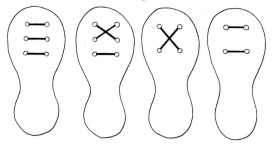

- Take some foot measurements for each child (length, width, girth/area.) Explore any links between these and age, height, shoe size.

	length		width		area		shoe size	height	age
	right	left	r	l	r	l			
Nikki	13cm	14cm							

Science/Design and Technology
- Can children recognise objects using only bare feet? Talk about textures, shape, size and weight of objects.
- Make footprints by dipping feet in talcum powder and printing on dark paper. Use these to discuss and label parts of the foot (ball, instep, heels, toes). Which parts touch the ground when walking, skipping, hopping or jumping?
- Compare treads of old and new shoes, boots and wellies. Test out the 'grip factor' on different surfaces and record the results.
- Research using books, X-rays and by children feeling their own feet, the bones and muscles in the foot. Use straws, polystyrene pieces, paper rolls to make pictures/mobiles of skeleton feet.
- Make foot care leaflets (such as those distributed from a health centre) showing children the importance of washing and drying feet, cutting nails and properly fitting shoes.
- Design and make: a shoe box; a flip-flop/slipper to fit anybody in the class; a practise lacing card.

Humanities
- How do shoes get to the shops? Find out where shoes can be bought locally (either visit a shoe shop/factory or use the Yellow Pages). Display the sequence from shoe to shop on a track of cut-out foot print shapes.

- Using pictures and your footwear collection, compare old and modern shoes. Think about use of materials and fashion ideas. Add speech or thought bubbles to the pictures - are the shoes comfortable, heavy, warm, difficult to put on? Place on a simple timeline showing feet walking along a pavement. Include a prediction for a shoe of the future.
- Investigate shoes around the world. Look at how climate and materials may affect design. Have any shoes special purposes?
- Make a 'Did You Know?' display showing interesting aspects of the history of footwear. You could include information, in picture/caption form, about: shoe trees, shoehorns, the shoe-shine boy, the derivations of footwear names (Wellingtons, platforms, winkle pickers etc).
- Make a chart comparing British, Continental and American shoe size measurements.

Art and Craft
- **Make tread patterns.** Children can either paint the soles of their shoes (make sure the paint washes off easily!) or make tread patterns using clay or Plasticine, thick card sole and string, wood off-cuts, polystyrene, fabric or anything that gives a raised effect. Match the treads to the shoes.

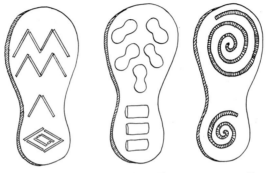

- Look at pictures drawn or painted with the feet. Try some yourself.
- Make a model of an alien's foot from construction toys, play dough, clay, papier mâché or junk materials.
- Look at pictures and paintings of foot decorations: painted with mendhi patterns, highly embroidered footwear for dancers, use of bobbles and bells. Children can decorate their own feet in a particular style or make pictures.
- Make some stilts out of carpet roll inner tubes.
- Make a close observational drawing of a shoe showing top and side view. Label the various features (sole, heel, uppers, eyelets, stitching).

Music
- Make up a shoe action song to the tune of 'Aiken Drum', e.g. 'Katie runs in trainers —- all around the room' (creeps in slippers, stamps in wellies, etc).
- Use percussion instruments to play patterns which suggest walking, skipping, jumping, leaping and running. Make footstep sounds go slowly, quickly, loudly, softly, coming closer, moving further away.
- Learn to sing: 'Slowly Walks my Granddad' (*Tinderbox* - A & C Black); 'What's Afoot?' (*Silly Aunt Sally*, Ward Lock Educational).

Further activities from the book
- Play a cumulative memory game: 'I went shopping with Gogo and we bought ...' Start from the items Songololo and Grandma bought together, then add your own.
- Look for all the sound words in the book (crying, shouting, barking etc). Add to these to make a poem of city sounds, e.g. mad cars honking/ tired baby crying/ lost dogs barking/ train driver shouting.
- Talk about why Songololo's Grandma has trouble walking. Design a really comfortable pair of shoes for Gogo.
- Songololo was Shepherd's nickname. Have the children got nicknames, and how do they feel about them? Share stories about how children got their nicknames from family or friends.
- By drawing on children's experience of places they have visited, newspapers, magazines, banks, or relatives living overseas, match countries with their currencies. Change £1 into other currencies and present as a conversion table.

Toys

DOGGER, Shirley Hughes (Little Greats, Random Century)
Peabody, Rosemary Wells. **Alpaca,** Rosemary Billam. **Tilly's House,** Faith Jaques.
Lady Daisy, Dick King Smith.

Collections

New and old toys of all kinds: jigsaws, soft toys, Turtle, Roamer or other robotic toys, computer games, board/card games, toys that float, make a noise or light up. Toys powered in different ways: spring, clockwork, magnetic, pull-along, motor, electric.

Starters

Brainstorm ideas about what toys are. Does a toy have to be bought, last for a long time, or just be fun to play with? Does Plasticine, piece of string, crayon, count? Use your collection to talk about stereotypes - do both girls and boys want to play with the same toys? Is it only very young children who have toys - what about adults? Talk about how the children amuse themselves at playtimes, after school and in the holidays. Make a picture list of game suggestions for friends. Take a straw vote on favourite toys and games used in class. Visit museums, toy library, local collections.

English

● Write labels for 'Our favourite cuddly toys' display. Ask the children to bring in their favourite soft toy for the day. Make labels to accompany the toys, concentrating on characterisation. Information on the labels could include: name and how this came about; special characteristics (moody, funny, helpful, kind); what makes it special; adventures survived. (See photograph.)

● Think about what somebody you know well would like as a toy. Check your ideas with that person. **Display as a gift tag** showing who the present is for, what it is and why the person would particularly like it.

● Retell one of the toy stories from the toy's point of view. Sequence major events with speech/thought bubbles.
● Give instructions for a game you know well - orally, as a flow chart, or a picture sequence.
● Make an inventory of class toys and games. Give it an alphabetical index or make it into a directory showing where in the room the toys can be found. Older children could extend this by using pictures and advertisements to make a toy catalogue.
● Promote a new toy. On the brochure give its name, price, appearance, what it does, and special features to encourage parents/children to buy it.

Maths

● Survey children's most popular toys. Show as a pictogram. Think about things like: does teddy have a heading of its own or will it go under 'soft toys'? Would 'wheeled toys' be a useful heading? Alternatively, choose five games found in class. Each child puts them in order of preference from 1 to 5. Collect data and chart most/least popular of the five.
● Sort toys/pictures and consider: how they are powered; whether they make a noise; have wheels/legs/wings; can be steered; materials; suitable age range.
● Take a programable toy (Roamer/Turtle) from place to place, e.g. a dog to the kennel, a car to the garage. Make sure children understand how to program instructions in a logical sequence.
● Roll a die. How often does each number come up? Make a frequency table to show your findings. Does it make any difference how many times you throw?

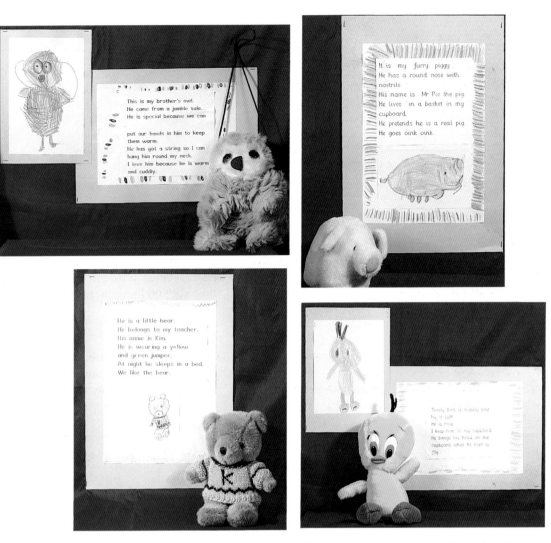

- Look at toy prices in a range of magazines and catalogues. Chart toys that are priced at less than/more than 50p, £1, £2 ... which is the cheapest/most expensive toy? What is the greatest number of toys you can buy for under £5 to fill a get-well goody bag?
- Over a week, log television advertisements for toys. Interpret the data, thinking about which toys were advertised and when. Make a longer term survey noting any seasonal differences (pre-Christmas, school holidays).

Science/Design and Technology
- Have a toy repair shop. Find toys and games in the classroom which need repairing. Think about: how to make missing cards/pieces for games; envelopes for jigsaw pieces; most appropriate repair materials. When is it best to use adhesive tape, PVA glue, screws, nails? Try making new clothes for toys. Carry out repainting jobs. Make new wheels and axles.
- Using junk materials make a pull-along trolley for a soft toy to ride in. Think of different ways of moving it along (wheels, rollers, runners). How can you make it move smoothly?
- Play a game of magnetic fish. Use the same principle to move a card 'toy' through a maze.
- Devise a game using three skittles and a bean bag. How many players? How is it played and scored?
- Look at how toys are powered (battery, clockwork, pull-along - See Starters). Design a symbol - as on a manufacturer's box - showing what makes the toy move, e.g. an outline of a battery. Attach labels to the appropriate toys/pictures.

Humanities
- Make a personal toy history. Can the children remember/find out what they played with aged 1, 2 ... 7? Display as individual timelines on silhouette shapes of their favourite toys for each year.

● Find out which toys that children play with now were also available to parents and grandparents. Are there any toys we have now that were not available to older people? Which toys have we all used? Record the information something like this:

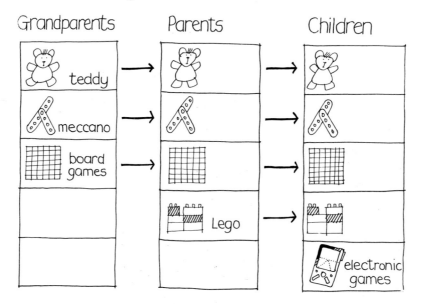

● Find out about playground games the children use now. How old are these games and how have they been passed on? Invite community members in to teach the children their favourites. Are any of these games still played? Make a tape of dips, skipping rhymes and singing games.
● Where are toys sold locally? Make a toy guide showing which shops sell toys and how much they cost. Include shop name, opening times, position, simple map.
● Look at 'labels of origin'. Trace where toys have been made. Can you spot any patterns? Where are most electrical toys made? In how many countries have teddies been made?

Art and Craft
● Use old construction toys/defunct games pieces to design and print wallpaper for a play house or covering for a toy box.
● Look closely at Bruegel's 'Children's Games'. Discuss the use of detail, movement and perspective. Make your own busy class frieze in the same style but of modern games.

● **Explore patterns made by toys like Spirograph.** Ask the children to make and cut out their own simple card shape. Pin to paper with a fastener. Draw round it. Turn the shape and draw round it again. Experiment with different rotating patterns. Fasten the shape in a different position.

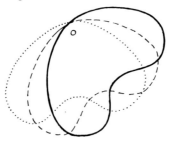

● Choose a small number of toys for children to make a pleasing arrangement. Draw/paint this still life. Encourage groups to look at and paint the arrangement from different angles.

Music
● Look at the way toys move: spin and glide, smoothly and lightly. Try out the movements. Match a percussion instrument to a toy, e.g. make a jerky pattern for a robot using a guiro, or use a hand whisk for a clockwork toy, starting quickly and getting slower.
● Learn the chorus of 'The Marvellous Toy' (*Sing a Song 1,* Nelson). Substitute the toy sounds (zip, bop, whirr) for some of your own. Then leave the words out and introduce instruments to make toy sounds.
● Listen to short extracts from 'The Fantastic Toy Shop' (Rossini/Respighi), or part of the Nutcracker/Coppelia suites. Which toys might fit the sounds or patterns heard?

Further activities from the book

● Make a 'treasures' book of toys or objects which are as comforting/precious to the children as Dogger.

● Look at and discuss the Fancy Dress Parade spread in *Dogger*. Use some of these ideas to design costumes to dress up your soft toy collection.
● Look through *Dogger* and talk about what some of the characters might have felt like at different stages of the story. What did Dave feel like when he had to go to bed without Dogger? What did Mum and Dad feel like when searching for him? Choose one aspect of the story and illustrate a character with a speech/thought bubble, showing what they were thinking at the time.
● Make a board game based on the summer fayre. Have bonus/forfeit squares showing things like: win the raffle - move on 2; long queue at the tea stall - miss a turn.
● Look at the stall Dogger was on. Have your own soft toy sale. Make everything in the shop 2p (or lp, 5p, l0p) to practise repeated addition, and use a calculator.

For details of further Belair publications,
please write to :
BELAIR PUBLICATIONS LTD.,
P.O. Box l2,TWICKENHAM
TWI 2QL ENGLAND.